THE WORKING DIRECTOR

HOW TO ARRIVE, THRIVE, AND SURVIVE IN THE DIRECTOR'S CHAIR

CHARLES WILKINSON

Published by Michael Wiese Productions
11288 Ventura Blvd, Suite 621
Studio City CA 91604
Tel. (818) 379-8799
Fax (818) 986-3408
mw@mwp.com
www.mwp.com

Cover Design: Michael Wiese Productions
Layout: Gina Mansfield
Editor: Paul Norlen

Printed by McNaughton & Gunn, Inc., Saline, Michigan
Manufactured in the United States of America

Library of Congress Cataloging-in-Publication Data

Wilkinson, Charles, 1952 March 2-
   The working director : how to arrive, thrive, and survive in
the director's chair / Charles Wilkinson.
        p. cm.
   ISBN 1-932907-02-5
   1.   Motion pictures--Production and direction--Vocational
guidance. 2.
Television--Production and direction--Vocational guidance. I.
Title.
   PN1995.9.P7W55 2005
   791.4302'33'023--dc22

2004012795

ACKNOWLEDGMENTS

Many people contributed to the experiences this book is based on. Writers, actors, other directors, producers, distributors, critics, agents, publishers, crews, mentors, students, friends, and family. In no real order: Allen Epstein, Catherine Lough Hagquist, Linda Saint, Anemone and Martin Schliessler, Ken Gord, Jim Green, Jerry Wasserman, Melissa Gilbert, Lee Dintsman, Don S. Williams, Adrian Paul, John Juliani, Pierre Trudeau, Barry Perelman, Henry Winkler, Lenka Svab, Dave Hardon, Sgt. Don Hanson, Tobias Schliessler, Crawford Hawkins, Mark Bacino, David Hauka, Jennifer Clement, Bruce Weitz, Harry Barber, Cal Schumiatcher, Gordon Pinsent, my brothers Lorne & Will. My parents Jack and Hazel.

—•—

Most of all: Nadya, Pablo, Fabio, and Tina.

For my Dad

TABLE OF CONTENTS

INTRODUCTION

"You directors, the second you turn in a picture that doesn't work, it's 'art' this and 'integrity' that. I hire and fire you bums like extras."

My first job interview

This book is not about where to put the camera.

It's not about the great masters of the cinema.

This book is about one thing: being hired to direct film and television.

More to the point, this book is about how to make that happen. It's about how to keep it happening and how to jump start when it falters. It's not that where you put the camera is unimportant or that the masters aren't worthy of study. It is and they are. *The Working Director* is going to talk about a different aspect of your craft.

A tiny percentage of film directors are "A" directors. The blockbuster helmers. An even smaller number are "auteurs" who write, produce, and direct their own work. The rest of us, as we hopefully work our way towards "A" director status, are *employees*.

We're hired to direct movies, TV films, episodes, documentaries. Sometimes the show turns out well. Sometimes not. You'd think that if your show turned out well you'd be off and running. Beyond the need of career advice. You'd think that. Truth is, short of a 50 million dollar weekend or an Academy Award™, no matter how the show turns out we're up against serious competition for *every* directing job. And there are things we do or neglect to do every day that affect our chances of being hired.

That's what *The Working Director* is about.

There are a number of terrific books on the world of the "A" director. At present there is very little by way of published discussion on the world of the successful *hired* director.

Yet as I say, 95% of the directors working at any given time are employees. And the rules we work under are vastly different from those in the "A" director's world. The "A" director has, within the context of the film, a power so absolute it approaches that of ancient kings. In the hired director's world the *Producer* has that power. Including the power to hire you. Or not. That makes a world of difference.

For example: In the "A" director's world the lead actors are cast (which is to say *hired*) by you the director. Their allegiance is to you. In the hired director's world the lead actors are most often hired by the producer. They are frequently more important to the financing than you are. Their allegiance is to their role or the producer or their public. But not necessarily to you. This book is about acquiring techniques for finding your place in this mix and using those tools to do the good work you must do.

Another example: As an "A" director you have wide powers over the script. You can make changes as you deem necessary. As a hired director it's not at all uncommon for producers to discourage the changing of a single word. *The Working*

Director is about acquiring techniques for getting the script changes you need to tell the story without risking unnecessary conflict.

The Working Director follows a linear format leading from a discussion of that all important first phone call on through prep, production and post, right up to getting your next and better job.

But you ask, *Why worry about it if my phone's ringing now?*

Because the competition for our job is, well... stiff. Consider this: there are over 6,600 universities in 175 countries world wide. The few that don't have film schools are more than compensated for by the several hundred more colleges and dedicated institutions that do. That's about how many film schools there are in the world. Every one of those schools is going to graduate at least one promising person each year who knows the basics of the job and would quite literally give body parts to be a director. That's *six thousand potential new directors every year...*

Here's another way of looking at it. The English-speaking cinema produces over 500 theatrically released feature films each year. Of those, fewer than 50 do so well that their director moves up to any kind of "A" status. That means 450 directors with recent theatrical credits are going to be looking to move down into the lower budget or TV slot you're looking to move up into.

Why do so many people want to direct?

Because directing is the best job in the world. Bar none.

Imagine.

Your phone rings. A script arrives at your door. A good one. A check arrives by courier. A big one. A driver picks you up in a car. A new-smelling one. These people in this office are nice to you. Really nice. You chair meetings. Interesting, harmonious, creative meetings. Everyone listens to you. A crew of capable workers assembles. They jump at your invitation to collaborate. A group of talented actors appears before your eyes. They accept you into their sandbox. You say the magic word, "*Action.*" Everything springs to life. Every fiber of your creative energy flows into the creation of a stream of images and sounds that, when placed in front of millions of viewers, provokes thought, laughter, tears, inspiration even. The critics rave. Flowers arrive at your door. You've just made your mark on history.

It gets that good and better. The best job in the world. Period.

Or not. Consider scenario B.

Your phone rings. A script arrives at your door. It "needs work." The people in the office are civil. To your face. You attend meetings. Fractious, inconclusive, angry meetings. People listen to you. Then they do it the way they feel like doing it. A crew of workers assembles grudgingly. A group of yesterday's actors appears before your eyes. One or more won't come out of their trailer. You say the magic word, "*Action.*" Everything limps to life. Every fiber of your creative energy (except those fibers devoted to watching your back) flows into the creation of a stream of images and sounds that, when placed in front of millions of viewers, provokes a "mixed response." The critics pan it. No flowers, no friends, no history. Just rumors that there were "problems" on set. You may not be working for a while.

It gets that bad and worse. Everything is so volatile. Make a few key mistakes and see how fast scenario A becomes scenario B. Make some good catches, have a few heart to hearts with the right people, connect with, even *galvanize* the unit, and B becomes A.

We work in a pressure cooker. Even a small unit costs someone a huge amount of money to run every day, every hour. Money that everyone on set knows *your* work must convince an audience to part with. We have weather pressure, time pressure, creative pressure, interpersonal pressure, tribal pressure, *tire* pressure for God's sake (a blown tire can cost an hour, a day, a human life). We work under the pressure of insanely long hours. Frequently in demanding, uncomfortable places. We suffer the pressure of days, weeks, months living, eating, working like sardines in a can with large groups of strangers. And when it's finally over we often suffer the gnawing pressure a telephone creates by simply not ringing.

Best job in the world when things go right. When they don't, a not so great job. Seasoned director or emerging hopeful, the script arrives at your door and you take your chances. Luck of the draw.

Or is it?

If you're going to take credit for how well scenario A works out doesn't that mean you kind of have to accept at least some of the blame for how badly scenario B unfolds?

Yes.

Is there anything you can do to prevent scenario B from happening again?

Yes.

Will you find answers in these pages?

Yes.

Some you'll already know. Many are self-evident. Some you won't agree with. And some are just real hard to practice. But hopefully some of the ideas you find here will get you focusing on aspects of your craft you've never considered before.

A note on gender language. "He/she" is awkward. "They" is often worse. Our business has made tremendous gains in the area of gender equality. Women and men are largely interchangeable and receive equal pay. So I will arbitrarily refer to a DP for example as "her" or "him" for the sake of flow without meaning to imply that DPs are all female or all male.

Some of what I have to say is aimed at emerging directors. And I'll note that where appropriate. Some of what I have to say is aimed specifically at established professionals. But the bulk of what follows is meant for the working director. Whether it's your first show or your hundredth. Because until you achieve "A" status, the rules are the rules.

But you say, *my talent is all I need. As long as I make good films, good TV, none of this other stuff matters.*

Experience suggests otherwise.

"A" status mostly doesn't last. When the Oscar-winning blockbuster delivering directors strike out a few times they're back to being employees. When the *auteur* director with a couple of well-reviewed smaller films fails to deliver festival success with later offerings, most of the time they will move into the working director realm. Of the few who persevere a new Jim Jarmusch will emerge from time to time and the rest will simply fade away. Scan the film festival lists from just five years ago. *Imdb.com* search the directors. See for yourself.

The fact is that directors who continue to work tend to be advice takers. We seek out every scrap of knowledge on how to ply the craft to get the absolute maximum out of our people and avoid the destructive and time-wasting landmines our projects are seeded with.

Film is an intensely social medium. Directors are by definition "people people." The cliché of the brooding loner who appears on set, does the magic silently and departs in mystery is generally a myth. Most directors talk a lot. They have to. There are so many choices. Brown hat or black? Mercedes or BMW? 85mm or 50mm? Sadder or happier? Bigger or smaller? Chocolate or vanilla. Literally *thousands* of questions a day. Certainly there are directors who delegate most of these choices. The AD can direct the actors. The cinematographer can come up with a workable shot. The teamster can decide whether Thelma and Louise drive a classic T-Bird or the rusty Honda Civic he wants to rent to the production. Somebody always says. Somebody always chooses. Thousands of choices a day. And each one of those choices has the potential to come back to slam us.

And if you say, *"All I have to do is do good work and nothing else matters,"* how exactly is good work measured?

Yes, a multi-million dollar opening weekend is a no-brainer. But frequently the success of our shows is very difficult to measure. What if you've just directed episode #6 of this season's 22 episodes of *Friends*? How do you measure that? Weekly ratings don't really measure *you*. It's not like they advertised the episode as being *un film de* you. Similarly, network executives and producers don't always credit the directors for the good ratings of their TV movies or mini-series. They speak instead of how the concept scored. Or the cast or the line-up. The only time TV is anything close to a director's medium is for those few brief moments on Emmy night. What about theatrical features? The industry leaders, to their credit, acknowledge that many factors create a success or failure at the box office. Cast, timing, script, promotion, what else is running. So the director of an unsuccessful theatrical is often given a second or third chance. Often, *but not always*. If not upon success then what is that decision to hire and re-hire you based on?

That is precisely what *The Working Director* is about. Getting work, doing work, getting more work.

Because to a director, not working is a slow death. You must work. Forget the money (sure you also must eat but if that was what it was about you'd have gone to dentistry school, not film school). Forget whatever prestige might come with the job. You direct because you love to tell stories. You live for the look in your audience's eyes when your voice drops to a hushed whisper and you say, "... *She crept through the dank and glistening tunnel, an ominous breathing all about her, when suddenly... BOOM!!!*" And they jump, scream, laugh, and forget for a moment their mean science teacher or their overdue car payment or what the doctor said that afternoon.

That moment is something that exists between you and your audience. That more than anything else is the pay check you receive for the work you do. But to get to that moment, to be able to repeat that moment with any regularity you have to thread your way through some very complex mazes. You have to get the job. You have to do the job well. You have to make the friends who will hire you to do the job again.

This is what *The Working Director* is going to talk about.

Who is he to talk, you ask?

If there was an Award category for *Dumbest Mistake on a Film or Television Show* I'd have a case full of golden statues. I've passed on major projects because I thought the shooting location was wrong. I've turned down highly paid work in Paris to help with a sound mix on a previous, troubled film. I've put myself between screaming executives and decent crew members. I've challenged corrupt film distributors who had numerous other shows they would otherwise have hired me for. I've told network executives poised to hire me that what I really wanted to do was features. I've spent years asking the wrong people for the right things on and off set. I've made mistakes. I've lived to tell the tale.

My first job in the entertainment business was at the age of three. I had an imaginary radio show. I'd sing myself to sleep for hours every night. By the time I was six my big brother and I actually were regular singers on a popular radio show. We graduated to TV as series regulars on a popular variety show, recorded, toured. All before I was fourteen. So I pretty much grew up chasing that moment. The moment the audience forgets everything and is just *with* you.

I went to film school. Before graduation I directed a documentary that won a few awards. I was hired by a small studio to direct another documentary far away from any supervision. I made the documentary — and secretly shot an impromptu feature at the same time with the same crew and the same budget. The documentary made a profit. The feature got a small theatrical release, scored mixed reviews, and my phone started ringing.

Since then I've directed four theatrically released features. All of them play regularly on late night TV. I've directed a number of well-received TV movies for the major networks, numerous episodic shows, and documentaries. I've written screenplays that others have directed. I've said no to projects that felt wrong. I've weathered periods of unemployment and equally challenging periods of prosperity. I've supported a terrific family. Together we've made a lot of extremely complex home movies on camping road trips to Mexico.

My phone has kept ringing.

Not because I've won an Oscar (I haven't). Not because I have Emmies (I don't). Not because I'm a push-over to work with (I'm not).

Producers hire and keep hiring working directors like me and you for a list of reasons so long it would fill a book.

Here it is.

chapter ONE

SETTING UP SHOP

AREA CODE

You've seen the medical shows that feature millions of sperm cells swimming upstream vying to be the one that penetrates the egg. That's the working director.

In the film business there's an extreme degree of competition to break in at even the lowest level. Once inside, the real competition begins. The director's job is seen as the ultimate goal. Achieving that goal requires skill, talent, and determination. It also requires a high degree of speculation, forecasting, risk taking, and educated guessing. And in the end for each project only one competitor succeeds. The target you're aiming for is very, very small. So the first logical consideration is — where exactly is the target?

While the undisputed world capital of English language mainstream filmed entertainment remains Hollywood, an ever increasing percentage of production takes place outside California. The development of inexpensive and highly portable production tools, the spread of filmmaking education, and the advent of the 500-channel universe have created viable production centers in many cities around the world. Increasingly it is becoming possible for directors to work prolifically without ever going to Hollywood. And even if a career in Hollywood remains the ultimate goal, the preferred method for breaking in has become the non-Hollywood production.

WHERE IS THE WORK?

Much of this first section will be known and understood by the more established directors. You seasoned directors may want to pretend it's a spec script from your neighbor's best friend and skim.

London, New York, Sydney, Vancouver, Munich, Paris, Montreal, New Orleans, Hong Kong, Bombay, Toronto, Rome, Prague, and more. All cities that produce programming for international exhibition. There are many directors in these centers who work day in, day out. And there are directors who work for a time in these places, then take their credits to Hollywood hoping that the talent they've demonstrated will put them ahead of the crowd. The first task is to find out who's shooting what and where.

How do you find out? There are many ways, some very simple. The Directors Guild of America (DGA) knows where every union show in the US is being shot, as does the International Alliance of Theatrical Stage Employees (IATSE), and the Screen Actor's Guild of America (SAG). They have availability lists, production lists, all kinds of info. They make the info freely available to their thousands of members. And even if you don't have a card it's not exactly top secret.

In Canada, the Director's Guild of Canada (DGC) maintains offices in all of the major regions. In Britain, BECTU has the info.

What do you need to know?

Where are they shooting the kind of show you're most likely to get hired onto?

Is there a **trend** at work? Is production increasing or decreasing? Why?

Why are they shooting there? Are there local tax breaks? Is it non-union?

Who are they hiring to direct? From where are they hiring them?

Are there **local restrictions** on who can be hired to direct?

RESTRICTIONS/PERKS

Some jurisdictions make use of local incentives to attract and stimulate development of a film industry. Often these incentives include some type of point system for the key creative personnel. That's us. Their idea is to encourage the production company to hire as many locals as possible.

It is critical for you to establish if this is a factor in the area where you wish to work. If so there may be a simple solution. Consider becoming a local. Some directors attempt this as a sort of scam and they're frequently met with resentment. On the other hand those who approach it by truly becoming a part of the local arts community are frequently welcomed. After all, what community wouldn't want a talented, high-income artist as a member?

Even where there's no official residency requirement it can still be an issue. Are one or more shows you feel you're qualified for shooting in New Orleans this season? Are the production companies flying their directors in? Is your aunt's best friend a New Orleans resident? Does she have a spare room? That makes you a local. You just saved the production company airfare and hotels. To a producer who is shooting in New Orleans for economic reasons, *that's* an incentive.

International co-productions have become a considerable source of quality work. Co-pros always have nationality requirements for their directors. Which rules you out, right? Not necessarily. Was your father born in England or France or Spain or wherever? How about your grandmother? Get in touch with the consulate. Find out what their rules are regarding repatriation and joint citizenship. You never know. Maybe you're entitled to a Euro card. Which is going to increase your chances of being a working director.

If you're not a U.S. citizen but wish to be eligible for directing jobs in the U.S., get a green card. Enter the official green card lottery right now. Today. Go.

The camera crew with Charles on The Highlander
Charles Wilkinson photo

GUILD AFFILIATION

All major production centers have union agreements in place. Which for the director means guild membership. A guild card won't get you a job. Nobody gets hired because they have a card. But sometimes not having the right card can affect your ability to work.

Low-budget shows often fly under the radar. They are seen as a means of breaking in. The guilds and unions tend to look the other way. The higher budget shows in Hollywood simply purchase DGA membership for their first timer. But for the bulk of the projects the working director needs to join the appropriate guild.

Generally a DGA card works pretty much everywhere. The reality is that U.S. companies have produced so much work in so many international jurisdictions and have brought so many DGA directors in to do those shows that there are agreements in place almost everywhere for DGA directors.

To work in Canada you need membership in the DGC. In Britain a BECTU card does the trick. But the DGA has negotiated reciprocal agreements with these Guilds and few countries will risk driving away lucrative U.S. production by enforcing their labor laws. So a DGA card usually gets you a work permit in Canada or Britain.

Joining the DGA is uncomplicated. You need to be hired to direct by a DGA signatory producer and pay the initiation fees and yearly dues.

Membership in the DGC is somewhat different in that besides initiation and dues it requires that the applicant has directed a minimum number of hours of dramatic programming (not necessarily guild signatory) and be recommended by a member in good standing.

Check out:

> U.S.A. — dga.org
> Canada — dgc.ca
> Great Britain — bectu.org.uk
> Australia — asdafilm.org.au
> New Zealand — sdgnz.co.nz

THE AGENT

Do you have the right agent? Should you look for a better one? Do you need an agent at all? Consider this: Virtually every director finds and signs their first life changing deal *without the aid of an agent*. That first low-budget movie. The first music video that lights the kindling that starts the fire that will become your career. No agent on earth can light that fire for you. Nobody in the directing trade gets "discovered." BUT, once you start a merry little blaze no one can turn it into a roaring bonfire like a good agent. So if your excuse for not working is that you have the wrong agent or no agent at all, that may be just what it is. An excuse.

If you're not currently working it's because the people doing the hiring aren't thinking about you. Or they're thinking the wrong things about you. Assuming you are qualified for the work, the right agent may be able to change this situation. But how do you get the right agent? By being a promising director. And how do you do that?

Direct. Wherever you can. Do a play that gets good notices. Do a music video for a group about to break out. Do a commercial on spec, a student film, a wedding. Enter every festival under the sun. Win an award. Suddenly the agent sees you (and more importantly can *sell* you) as the award winning director who just....

Can the Right Agent Get You Work?

Sometimes. If you are studio or network approvable for the kind of work you want and if your agent is in that particular loop then yes, they can. What does that mean?

If you've directed 20 episodes of prime time drama and if your agent talks daily with the producers who hire for prime time drama then your agent can probably get you more of the same kind of work. Can that agent get you a studio feature? Almost certainly not.

On the other hand let's say you have one low-budget feature to your credit. Say it didn't go theatrical but a few critics liked it and it won some awards. Can an agent who's plugged into the world of small features get you serious job interviews for more of the same? Yes. Can that agent get you on to this season's hot prime time episodic? Almost certainly not. Agents specialize.

GM Goodwrench mechanics know nothing about fixing Ferraris. They never see one. Likewise, the perfectionist Ferrari mechanic wouldn't know where to start on that $49.95 tune-up.

Directors often complain about their agents. The agency is too small. Nobody takes their calls. Or they're too big. They don't take *your* calls. Or they're addicted to packaging. They claim your name doesn't have the sizzle that the latest ex-rocker first timer's does. The complaints may very well be true.

But the complaints we make about our agents are often excuses.

Put yourself in the agent's place. They can't stay in business if they don't have income. In a way an agent is like a salesman. Give a salesman a desirable product and they'll move it. As anti-art as it sounds, if you make yourself that desirable "product" your agent will sell you.

Big vs. Small

Everybody wants to be repped by the CAA, ICM, or the William Morris Agency. They rep the biggest of the big. Some of that success is bound to rub off on you, right? And also, their sweatshirts are cool. Who doesn't enjoy a visit to the park with "Property of Wm. Morris" on their chest? And their logo on your resume and demo reel. What producer won't put that one at the top of the pile?

Pure fantasy.

I was represented by the Morris Agency for two years. I worked, but not one of my jobs came from them. Why?

Because the kind of work I was approvable for was simply not going to Morris clients. And of the few jobs my agent there could have sold me for, he had other clients with better credits. When I came to my senses and signed with an L.A. agency that was tops in *my* field my phone started to ring again.

Was I wrong to sign with Morris? No. Besides directing I write spec screenplays. During the time I was there two or three of my scripts were seriously looked at by people who could have helped them happen if the material was right. That chance, however slim, was worth something.

My point? The big/small criterion isn't the way to choose an agent. So what is?

Here's a way I've found that works. Pick a number of shows you realistically could have been, but weren't, considered for. Find out who directed them and who represents those directors. Call these agents. Tell them who you are. Ask for a meeting. If you've been truly realistic regarding where you stand a chance of being hired, odds are the agents will want to meet you.

Here's another method that can work very well. Say you've found the agent that's perfect for you. Only problem is they don't want to sign you just now. What to do?

Bring *them* your best lead. Do the agent's job for them. Find a job you are hirable for. Do the leg work. Call for yourself. Take the meeting. Again, if you were correct in your judgment about how hirable you are, the producer will talk to you without an agent being involved. Once it looks like they want you, go to the agent and ask them to close and commission what amounts to a done deal. In a way it's kind of bribery. But it also shows you're motivated. And most importantly it tells the agent that you take responsibility for your own career.

The same applies when you have an agent but you're considering a change. Don't wait until you're into a slow patch to shop around. Who wants to rep an unemployed director? Make the calls when you're working. Very few agents will refuse to meet a working director.

Bottom line, there are SO many agents out there. Every one of them is right for someone. Get the right one for you.

Speaking of bribery, *reward your agent*. Let them share in your excitement. Every time they get you work buy them flowers or a fruit basket. When they get you work in Paris send them a print from the Louvre. When they get you work in Germany, say it with *lederhosen*.

THE DEMO REEL

Who needs a reel? This year's Oscar winner doesn't. A director with one show doesn't. Pretty much everyone else does. The first and most important thing to consider is this: Who's going to be watching it? The producers of the shows you want to do. The studio people, the network execs, the distributors and their personal assistants. In other words, busy people. They may watch your reel with their thumb on the FF button while they're on the phone. Seriously. I've sat in rooms with producers while they watch other directors' reels like that. You have to bet they do the same with mine and yours.

What's going to make them take their thumb off FF? For some it will be a famous face or a wild action sequence or a love scene. Others will want to see scenes like the type of show they're producing. Funny scenes for a comedy. Dramatic scenes for a drama. So it's important you send a reel that's appropriate.

Demonstrating the Wrong Stuff

The environment they're watching your demo in is frequently not conducive to quiet reflection. There are tapes and head shots all over the desk, phones ringing, assistants in and out,

CNN running full time on one of the monitors, barely controlled chaos. They've got other director reels to go through. What are some sure-fire turn offs?

Wrong Genre: *"This is an action director, we're going for comedy."* Eject

Wrong Craft: *"Oh great, a montage of explosions, grins and kisses cut to the latest pop music. Give them a job as editor."* Eject

Too Short: *"Is that all they've got? This director lacks experience."* Eject

Too Long: *"Yeah, uh huh, got it already. What else they done? FF, no that's rewind, uh... wait, that's CNN."* Eject

Old Titles: *"Wow, I used to watch that when I was a kid. That director must be ancient..."* Eject

Poor Quality: *"What? Was that shot on a handycam?"* Eject

All bad.

Demonstrating the Right Stuff

A good reel tells them you can direct.

A good reel tells the people watching it that you can do *their show*. In this age of nonlinear editing every director with a home computer can make multiple versions of their reel.

A good reel is clearly labeled. It has your info and a table of contents on the box as well as on the tape/disc itself. A good reel has good scenes. It tells the viewer that full shows are available on request with a phone number right there.

A good demo reel impresses, wows, entertains. It gets you seriously considered. For what? You've moved to the right town. You've got an agent or you're working up to it. You've got a set of reels for all occasions. What's missing?

FINDING THE JOBS

The most certain route into the director's chair is to get yourself attached to a good script. It's not unheard of for the studios to take on a first-time director if their script is perceived to be hot enough. How do you get attached? Obviously, if you write your own script you're attached. But screenwriting is a dark art in its own right. Those directors wise enough to realize they can't write can still get attached to a terrific script. There are many unattached screenplays in the world. Thousands of new ones every day. Emerging screenwriters are highly motivated to get their work produced. Most cities have screenwriting groups and workshops. Drop by. Seek out the talent. Develop some relationships. There are thousands of credible producers who will take you on in a heartbeat if you bring them a viable project.

But most working directors are not attached to scripts. They simply get hired to do a job.

How Do You Find Out About These Jobs?

Most directors look for work most of the time. Even if your agent knows what's out there and has you up for it, that still leaves room for some potential work to fall through the cracks. Your agent may never hear of low-budget projects.

And yet there are many such projects you would be well to consider. Who wouldn't have directed *Blair Witch* on spec?

Producers are sometimes very secretive about their plans. Maybe they're in delicate negotiations with a star. Maybe they're having rewrite problems. Maybe they're holding out for union concessions. There are any number of reasons a producer wouldn't announce. Most of an agent's day is occupied trying to run these rumors to ground. They miss some. That's where you come in.

The second you hear of a real project that you might be right for, call your agent. If you know before they do they'll be happy you called. Even if they knew it lets them know you're on the job.

Your Guild office knows the minute a producer starts hiring office PAs. Stay in touch. Make certain they have your updated info. Make the occasional social call to your producer and production manager (PM) friends. Pay attention to the trades, the grapevine.

Less obviously, maintain your contact with the *headwaters*, the high mountain streams that will become raging rivers. Where is *that* at? It's not tough to foretell where the next hot filmmakers are going to come from. The film schools, the DV underground. All of these places have shows. You see their posters flapping on phone poles. All of these places have watering holes, bars, coffee shops. You as a working director are welcome in these places. Because you've got something they want. Credibility. You're a working director. And they have something you want. An inside track on tomorrow. Not to mention that the people in these places are a lot of fun to hang out with.

Say you're on friendly terms with the DV underground. Say you've helped a few of them hook up with equipment, supplies, introductions. Say one of the best and the brightest has a feature script. It's terrific. He has investors. The investors need to know the director can deliver. Who are they going to call? You.

To Schmooze or *Not* To Schmooze

In my experience industry parties, festival galas, schmooze fests don't get you work. They can be depressingly shallow celebrity-driven greed/envy lie-a-thons that make you wish you had chosen a career shepherding in the Pyrenees.

They can also be a venue to renew old acquaintances, eat great free food, drink expensive free liquor, and show the community that in spite of all the gossip to the contrary you're still alive and kicking.

Free food and liquor aside, there is some value in maintaining a presence in the community. And yes, it's *possible* someone will mention a project you could be right for. Just not real probable.

There's a Job Out There

Ultimately you beat the bushes, go to the parties, read the trades, overhear someone's cell call. You sniff out a job that sounds right. You get your name and material in front of the person who makes the hiring choice. Want to know something amazing? If you keep this up and have just an average amount of luck — they WILL call. Luck and perseverance.

Early on in my career I shamelessly pitched a producer who had a project way over my head. He didn't hire me. Over the years I kept pitching. He kept not hiring. I bumped into him one day, remembered I'd heard he was doing something new, again over my head. I pitched him anyway. Halfway through I stopped, smiled and said, *"You're never going to hire me, are you."* He smiled back and said, *"I just did."*

Congratulations, you've set up shop.

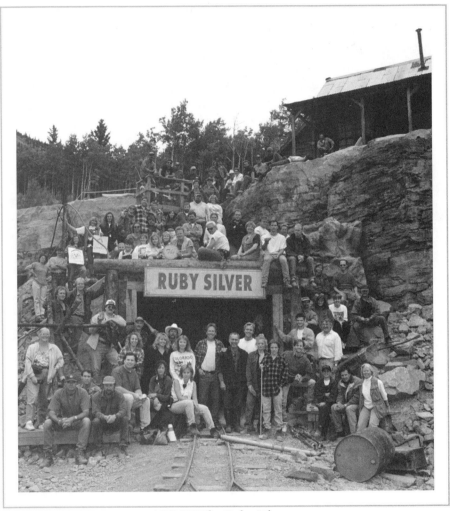

ABC-TV The Ruby Silver
Myrl Coulter Photo

chapter **TWO**

THE PHONE RINGS

"Hi, this is _____ calling about a project to see if you would be interested and available. Please get back to me..."

Every single call that comes in sparks a heart rate increase. It should. Some calls mark the beginning of the most wonderful projects. And some not. How do you tell which calls are which?

Your initial objective when answering the Phone Call is to establish three key things:

1. Is this job for real?
2. Is the project of interest? Do I want to do it?
3. Am I being offered a job? Or a chance to audition?

WHO'S CALLING?
By considering the source of the call you can make some assumptions about the potential job and how you should react.

If it's your agent telling you that studio/network/producer XYZ is interested in you for a project, chances are the project is real in the sense that there's a fair probability that the project meets basic industry standards and that you will likely receive an acceptable offer if you respond accordingly.

If the call is coming from a friend, a social acquaintance, or some person/company you've never heard of, it could be a vastly different story and may call for a different response.

One easy shortcut is to field your calls in front of your computer. As soon as they tell you their name, *Imdb.com* search them. A quick internet search won't tell you who they absolutely are but it may tell you who they're not.

What's the Status of the Job?

Is it green lit, "flashing green," in actual development, gasping for life, or one of the thousands of projects circulating around that will never go into production?

If the call comes from your agent they'll say something like, *"It's an HBO mini-series slated for the fall. They want you for three months starting in August."* There it is. Green lit. They'll want you to read the script and talk things over. If all that goes well you're as good as hired.

If your agent tells you it's "flashing green" that means the studio or network will greenlight it when the producer secures one or more key elements. Usually stars, often a decent re-write, occasionally the director. If they're talking to you at this point it likely means they believe you can assist them to get the green to go solid. You go in, meet their prospective star, pitch your take on the story, help the writer with the script, have lunch with the studio/network people and away you go. The down side is it's a lot more work, you don't get paid extra for it, and if the show performs poorly, you will take a larger than usual share of the blame. On the up side you get a project on which you're allowed meaningful input. No contest.

When the call comes from anyone other than your agent, a working producer, or a studio/network, some reliable method must be found to establish the current status of the project. I have developed a really subtle way of intuiting what's what with an unknown project. Within the first few minutes of the call I will ask, *"Is this project financed?"* If the answer is *"Yes, we go to camera in eight weeks,"* there it is, green lit. In other words you can now move on to focus on content. If the answer is *"It's a deferral picture. We all believe in the show so much we're doing it for points..."* that's not *necessarily* bad. More and more projects are going on a low or no budget basis to try and circumvent the star/studio system. There's nothing intrinsically wrong with doing a good show on spec. It's just important to know up front. More on this later.

What Are They Actually Saying?

Are they offering you the job or offering you a *chance to audition*? Again, if it's your agent and they're talking about dates, you know they intend to hire you unless you choose to pass.

But frequently what's being said (although not in so many big words) is, *"Let's talk. If you impress us we'll send you a script. If your take on the material impresses us and if the network/studio feels the same, it's yours."*

It's obviously REALLY important to quickly sense whether you're being offered the job or a chance to audition. If you pitch too hard on a job that's essentially yours you'll introduce doubt where none previously existed. Conversely, if you don't realize that you're auditioning you might create the impression that you're not all that interested.

So The Call comes in. You talk with them for a while. You learn what the project is, when, where, who. You also intuit how solid the people are. Why they're calling you, what they're actually saying to you, and what your chances of getting it are. If by this point both of you are still talking, chances are you're going to be reading the script.

THE SCRIPT ARRIVES
The script arrives, you sit down to read. What are you looking to find?

By the time you finish your first read of a script you should be able to say, *"Hey, what a good idea for a show."* If the script, however flawed, is built upon a good strong story, the director has something to work with. But if the story is weak it doesn't matter what you bring: great dialogue, terrific action, cool shooting and cutting. It won't be enough. This is a tough call to make when you need work. But you need to remember, the only thing worse than a hole on your resume is a horrible credit.

At the same time it's important to think these things through pretty carefully. When my agent sent me the script for the first *Air Bud* I said, *"A dog playing basketball? What kid's going to buy into that?"* Doh!

For now let's assume the script you've been sent falls somewhere between excellent and good.

"Hi, I Read Your Script and...."

Stop!

Remember back in grade school when the cute kid sitting two rows over sent you a Valentine card, *"Be mine."* You know they may have sent the same card to others. Your immediate goal became working up the nerve to pick up the phone and ask them if they'd go to the Valentine dance with you.

Now you've been sent a script. *Be my director.* You have to call them back. Before you pick up the phone, consider what school kids used to (and probably still) do. We'd *rehearse* the phone call for hours before making it. So what are you going to talk about?

"What's Your Take on the Material?"

They want to know if you get it and if you like it and if you think you can do a good job with it. In simple terms what makes this script special to you? Sometimes if you've been e-mailed the script your first reaction could take the form of a short reply e-mail. Just this morning I responded via e-mail to a script I received last night. My initial comment: *"It's a very good story. The script is developing it nicely, making me feel for the characters. This show has potential to be very entertaining."* The producers responded positively. We will now move on to the next level.

The next question you can count on being asked: *"Do you have any script notes?"* Of all the questions a working director must answer, this one is the trickiest. I try and see it from the producer's side. Frequently they've been through development for months already. They've sat through meetings with executives who may have made crippling script demands. Think they want more of the same from me? So... I should just say the script is brilliant and move on, right? Wrong. For two reasons. One small one and one big one. The small one is, most producers are smart people. They know their script isn't perfect. How impressed will they be if I don't notice? The big reason, you get what you settle for. The story may need minor changes as we go along. If I claim it's perfection now, how am I going to do my job?

So in planning the phone call I plan to talk about the elements that make the key story points work. The script I received last night is a feature about a woman discovering she was separated at birth from her identical twin. The twin is murdered. She sees the murder in a vivid dream. As a "witness" she becomes a target. There is a lot to like about the story. The central characters are strong and unusual. A murdered twin sister is a powerful inciting incident. The location, New Orleans, is exotic.

One of the notes I plan to make is that the lead character could be a bit more idiosyncratic. A bit more fun. This will remind the producers I'm interested in casting, character, and performance. It will give the producer a chance to jump in and either agree or display a penchant for over-controlling: *"Just not too idiosyncratic, okay?"*

Because I know the script is a first draft I'll plan to try to leave the door open to change. In this particular case my two biggest notes are that whoever the killer is, their overall motivation needs strengthening. Why did they kill the sister in the first place? In this case it was for money but at present the details are weak. I think that part needs developing. And secondly, given that the show is a "who done it" we need the revelation of the antagonist to be both surprising and inevitable. These are not major structural notes. But presented wrongly they could get our creative collaboration off to a bad start or worse yet, no start at all. I think I'm ready now.

THE CALL BACK

I've read the script, made my notes, booked the call. A few obvious notes. I disable my "call alert" function. It's distracting. I take the call someplace quiet and secure away from the kids and dogs. I have a pitcher of water standing by in case my throat goes dry. I take some deep breaths and punch the numbers. I'm on.

From this point forward I'll speculate on what I predict will happen when I call these producers back. It's speculation but this is how it usually goes.

They will ask for my take. I'll reiterate my "strong story, lots of potential" comment. They will ask about script changes. I'll feel my way through that.

They will want to talk about cast. They may have one or more lead roles cast as part of the financing. I'll make the call in front of my computer so I can search the actors I don't know. If and when they ask me my opinion I've got a few ideas I'm happy to share.

Tech Talk

There's a pretty good chance they'll want to get a quick reaction from me on the practical aspects of shooting in New Orleans. *"What do you feel about shooting it in six weeks?"* That sort of thing. I don't know yet what their proposed schedule is. But if they want to shoot this feature in eight days I need to know that right now. Or if they want 16-hour days, 7-day weeks. These are things I need to consider before proceeding further. Obviously some things are outright deal breakers. No point in wasting anyone's time. But it's good to be patient here. If they ask me if four weeks are doable, a good answer might be something like, *"Depends. If it's super well organized and you get the right crew and locations...."* Patience.

The call will draw to a close. I'll have a decision to make. Do I want the picture? The producers will have a decision to make. Do they want me? Let's cross our fingers and say the answer to both questions is yes. By the time you read this I will have met with the producers and gotten the job or not. If so, we'll have shot and posted. The reviews, box office and ratings will be in. It will be searchable on *Imdb.com*. So let's leave that one aside for now and carry on with the process.

PREPPING THE MEETING
> *"They want to meet you, it's just a formality."*
>
> > What agents say when there's a 50/50 chance you'll get the job.

The Meeting is critical. For the working director if the meeting goes well there's a high probability you'll be offered the job and you'll accept it. If it goes badly you either won't get an offer, you'll pass, or you'll end up taking a job you know in advance could have problems.

Ideally the first meeting is an opportunity for you and the producers to talk informally. To get a sense of each other. To get a feeling of how your and their approach to the project would mesh. *"Do we agree on the material, can we get along?"*

Directing Yourself in the Meeting

By now you've had a chance to analyze the Call Back. You've

reflected on how the producer responded to your pitch. You know that they responded well to a particular set of ideas you had. You know they responded less well to other ideas.

You've had a chance to study the script with this new knowledge. You sense where they want to go with the project. You may have some new script ideas. Possible solutions to problems identified during that conversation.

You have studied the characters. You've gained insights into them. It's always good to refer to the characters by their cast names. It shows you know the script.

You have some ideas about Cast. It's often worthwhile to refer to a role as Meryl Streep-*like* or Russell Crowe-*like*. The humor is always appreciated (think we can get him/her?) and it's a kind of shorthand.

You will also have formed some ideas about crew. One big discussion point will be the director of photography. Have some viable suggestions. No film school friends unless they have the credits to back it up.

You may have ideas about locations. If you are a local, here's your chance to show how well you know the area.

You will have formed some ideas about the style the picture should have. You will have opinions about lens choice, camera mode (handheld, etc.).

You have given thought to schedule issues: *"Three weeks in the city location, two weeks at the beach location, one week on a stage."* That sort of thing. Rough scheduling will also clue you in as to where the producer's coming from. If it's a

4-week TV movie with a lot of action sequences at sea during a storm, it's pretty obvious you're shooting in a wave pool with a significant 2nd unit out chasing weather. If it's an inexperienced producer who wants to do it all on location with main unit, be afraid. Be very afraid.

The Objective

Prior to going into the meeting you need to be clear with yourself about your own goal. If you want the picture no matter what, then that's your goal. Meet, shake hands, pitch, hope for the offer.

But often your goal will be dependent upon the producer's goal. Obviously if you get a sense that the producer's goal is to tuck a few hundred thousand into his jeans and let you take the rap from the critics, your goal becomes getting his assistant to validate your parking and getting gone. Alternatively if his goal is winning an Oscar or an Emmy, what a happy coincidence. Wouldn't it be great if you knew in advance what the producer's goal is? You can.

Imdb.com **the producer.** If they have a resume chock full of quality projects chances are they'll probably want quality this time as well. Likewise with the financing. If the money is from a quality source — a studio, a network, a respected distributor — you're very likely going to end up with a quality product.

My take on this is that there are four categories of producer. Award Quality, Quality, Emerging, and Sleaze. Award Quality speaks for itself. You've heard of them or their shows. They have awards. Quality is much more common. These are the vast majority of producers who produce the vast majority of quality shows. They generally pay their bills and keep their words. The Emerging producer is a tough call. All you can do is find out who else is part of their team, who's financing, and what's the script like? Sleaze is easy to spot. Their credits often start in the '70s with quasi porn/action titles, through the '80s it's bad action adventure that went straight to tape, in the '90s they jumped on the "family" fare bandwagon. In the new century they're scrambling for what they can get. Beware.

Follow the money. Find out who is financing the show. Is it a studio, one of the big networks, a small specialized network? Or is it mysterious "foreign money," an "investment syndicate," a known house of schlock?

If the money is coming from a reputable source it's no guarantee that the show will be good. But it should guarantee a minimum standard of behavior and quality. If the money is coming from a questionable source your odds are not good.

Pre-judging based on past behavior isn't always fair. And it's not always 100% accurate. But things add up. If the script is borderline bad, if the money is sleazy, if the producer has a history of dreck, you know where you stand.

What Are They Thinking About You?

Part of your preparation for the meeting is to prepare for *what they're thinking about you*. Remember they have *Imdb* too. They have telephones. They're bound to know some of the people you've worked for. They may have seen your work and read your reviews. They're going to have formed an opinion of you too. What is that opinion likely to be?

Play the devil's advocate for a sec. Put yourself in the producer's chair. Research *yourself*. Go over your resume. Be hard on yourself. Make the accusations. You're not experienced enough. You're too young or too old. You've never done comedy, or drama, or visual effects. You've never worked with a difficult star. You've never done an action show or a kid's show. Why aren't you famous?

What kind of picture emerges? What would a stranger intuit to be your strengths and weaknesses? When you walk into the meeting they're going to be looking at you from *that* point of view regardless of how true and accurate that picture of you actually is. You need to be able to speak to that. Part of your prep for the meeting involves coming up with short, positive answers to these questions.

I See By Your Outfit

What should a director look like? In a way it depends on the show, on the people you're meeting.

If it's a network prime time drama and you walk in with torn jeans, a cheap watch, and scruffy, graying hair they're going to think, *this old guy is not doing too well*. I had a meeting in L.A. with a large producer of episodics. L.A. traffic being what it is I had to race to get to the meeting. I was in an open car. I arrived with messy hair and windblown clothes. I was hoping maybe I looked kind of arty. People expect directors to be a little eccentric, right? Not in this case. I walked into their marble office. The Armani-clad, Rolex-wearing producer gave me a look and the meeting was essentially over.

On the other hand if you take a meeting with some promising newcomers who have a great, low-budget script and you walk in wearing an expensive leather jacket and a Rolex, their response could be: *too Hollywood*.

It's important to be yourself. But if you want the job your appearance should not be wildly at variance with the show.

Actor Gary Chalk, Charles, operator Will Waring, and DP David Geddes
Tina Schliessler Photo

Fashionably Late?

This isn't a cocktail party. 2 p.m. means 2 p.m. But being early creates a bad impression as well. Too eager.

What if *they're* late? William Goldman claims that if he's kept waiting more than fifteen minutes for a meeting he's out of there. It may work for him. I've tried it. I've lost work. It's a tough call. Chances are that it's a legitimate production emergency delaying the producer. Patience is probably best.

Ready? Here we go.

THE MEETING
The assistant shows you in. Hands are shaken. First looks are exchanged. Have a seat. Want something to drink? They may say some nice things about you. Be ready to reciprocate. What shows have they done that you admire? Praising them is not necessarily sucking up. You know the incredible hurdles *you've* jumped to be able to sit here in this room on this day and call yourself a director. The producer's feat is no less amazing. Respect the achievement. Respect the office.

Some producers can't wait to tell you how it is in *their* world. Others are interested in you. It becomes obvious fast. Some like lots of chit chat. Others want to talk turkey. Here's the good news: By this point you've done so much prep the meeting will unfold as it will.

Be prepared to have a conversation lasting anywhere from ten minutes to a few hours. When the producer talks don't just catch your breath. LISTEN. Nine times out of ten what they're trying to tell you is *how to get the job*.

There will be times when you'll be in a meeting and you'll realize this job is just not for you. But recognizing that this job is wrong for you doesn't mean your work is done here. You need to let them down *easy*. A little diplomacy is worth a lot. This particular project may not be your cup of tea but who's to say their next one won't be? A politically savvy Hollywood producer once told me:

> *"Everyone who isn't your friend... is your enemy."*

Jeez, that's an encouraging thought.

There will also be times when you really want the job but sense the meeting is going badly. It's often not that hard to intuit. Sometimes when I sense it's going against me, I'll say something like,

> *"I'm a good director. I relate very well to the actors. I get good performances. I motivate the crew to work quickly and well. I come prepared. I shoot efficiently. I rarely need overtime. I compose interesting shots that are also cuttable as coverage. I tell the story and my shows always play well. If I do your show it may be we'll get along and want to work together again. I have many repeat credits. It may be we won't hit it off. But the bottom line is, I'll direct an entertaining show that makes us all look good."*

This line has gotten me quite a lot of work. Because it's the truth.

Regardless of how well the meeting goes it's unusual to receive an offer on the spot. That can take days, sometimes weeks. Even longer. I try to think about something else. With my last meeting they promised to call back within the hour. They didn't. I got tired of looking at the phone. I used the time to learn "Blackbird" on the guitar. I finally made it through without a mistake. As the last notes were dying away the phone rang.

THE OFFER

> *"They called with dates."*
>
> The second coolest thing you'll ever hear your agent say.

An offer. Wow.

The manner in which the offer is made depends on the type of show it is. If it's a feature or network long form the offer will be negotiated back and forth between your agent and the studio/network. If the offer is for an episode on a series, again it will most likely be your agent doing the talking.

On a low-budget show where you are being asked to do the show for considerably less than guild scale, frequently the offer will be made directly to you. Even if you have an agent. It will be up to you to deal with it initially. But if you do have an agent you may want to consider having them negotiate the final details. More on that later.

On a "no budget" or spec show where you are being asked to work for no money, you'll be doing most of the work the agent normally does. And again it's worthwhile to get your agent to negotiate the final deal. The principle here is that low- and no-budget shows have a high mortality rate. If you waste a lot of your agent's time chasing down work they ultimately never get paid for, they're going to stop taking your calls.

Regardless of the type of show, the complexity of your negotiation is going to be a function of money. The more money involved, the more negotiating.

The Big Time

On a studio feature or a network long form there's a high probability you won't be working for scale (the guild negotiated minimum pay for a show of that type). Most directors who work at the upper end of the business are paid "over scale." How much over is a function of your past success and/or how much they want you. There's also an element of poker playing your agent and the producer will engage in. And let's be clear. This is agent country.

Besides your actual fee there's your final credit, your billing on posters and TV ads, your edit rights, your office (how luxurious), your trailer (how long), whether you get a driver or not, how and when you get your dailies, what kind of and how many final copies of the finished show you get, etc., etc. On top of all this, if it's a location show there are the potentially complex issues of accommodation, per diem, travel, travel tickets for your family, what kind of rental car, and on and on.

Sometimes the offer deals with these issues on a "favored nations" basis. In other words nobody on the show gets better treatment than you. But even then there may be some wiggle room. Let your agent be the bad guy. Just tell them what you need from the deal. As far as the money is concerned your agent needs to hear from you something like one of the following: *"I want this picture. Make the best deal you can, but don't blow it."* Or, *"I'm lukewarm about this show. If they don't come up with the right money, pass."* That type of thing.

When it comes to the details, improperly negotiated small things can become big very quickly. If the shoot is way over on the other side of the city, two hours of self driving every day is going to get old very quickly. Given how tired you're going to be in the later weeks it could also be dangerous. Ask that they negotiate a driver. While you're at it get your agent to negotiate a mini DVD player, negotiate your dailies on DVD, watch dailies on the ride home. It's in the production's interest that you get enough rest.

If the show is in Thailand and you need to fly there four times in prep and make several trips home during the shoot, your agent should negotiate first class airline tickets. Ten hours of cramped, crying baby, tourist class hell is not going to deliver you to set in any condition to work.

On a long location shoot accommodation is critical. A flea bag is okay for a night or two. So's a tent. But after two months of shooting you don't need external sources of stress. My general rule is that location accommodations should be of the same caliber as my home. I don't live in palatial splendor. I don't live in a dumpster. But I do live someplace interesting with a good kitchen. On a long shoot I need that.

Are they giving you a car? Same guideline. What kind of car do you drive yourself? If it's a beater whatever they give you is fine as long as it runs. If you drive a Ferrari that may be a tad excessive. Wouldn't you rather the money go up on the screen? If you're a car person, the production's rental outfit usually has a convertible or something interesting on hand. (As a side note, if you are unhappy with the car they give you ask the transport department. It's usually a point of pride for transport to find you an interesting ride for the same money.)

Need a phone? How about a computer? A bicycle? A health club membership? Video rentals? Tell your agent. But keep in mind that if your demands become excessive there are directors out there at a comparable level who'd do the job for scale.

EPISODIC
Virtually everything that applies to big project contract negotiation *doesn't* apply to episodic. There's very little to negotiate. Typically every director is paid scale. If the show is on location your agent may get a few extra dollars for per diem, maybe a slightly better car. Maybe you can get a digital master at the end. The watchwords with episodic are *favored nations*. If they give you a Porsche they have to give all the other directors a Porsche.

With episodic most of the negotiation is over schedule. You're busy in August and October. Can you do two shows back to back in September? That's what your agent is talking to them about.

LOW-BUDGET
There will be good shows you are offered that simply don't have the money to pay anything near the guild rate. But because of the script or the people you'll want to do the show anyway. Does that mean no negotiation? Not at all. There are

things they can give you instead of money. Like some form of producer credit. Like a piece of the back end (a percentage of the money the producer receives). These things can often be difficult to negotiate. You're frequently dealing with inexperienced producers. Once you've agreed in principle to do the show it's a good idea to have your agent take it from here.

If you don't have an agent it's often a good idea to find a novice (and therefore cheap) entertainment lawyer. You can bring them up to speed, then let them do the thing lawyers are good at: negotiation.

How Low Can You Go?

Occasionally you'll get an offer that seems offensive. Is it? Do they have the money or is the producer trying to chisel you? If you really like the project and need the work consider taking it on a "no quote" basis. In other words when the next producer calls your agent and asks what you last worked for, they can't divulge.

Spec

It is becoming more common for shows to be produced speculatively with very little cash financing. The promise is made that when the picture goes into distribution the cast and crew will be paid from the revenue the film earns. In theory it sounds great.

In practice this is how it tends to work. A distributor or network will advance money to the producers in return for the right to exhibit the finished show. When audiences start paying to see the finished show the distributors first subtract their sales commission, 30 – 40% of every dollar. Then they subtract all the expenses: prints and ads, publicity, travel, hotel, etc. Then they subtract the amount they originally advanced. The net result is that unless the picture is a runaway hit like *Blair Witch*, the distribution expenses and fees tend to gobble up everything. Very few workers on a spec film ever see any money.

There is one way a spec film can guarantee money back to the people who make the film. It's like an ancient whaling expedition where the 3rd harpooner was promised a 265th share in the catch. They'd whale for no wages. Then when the ship docked the blubber and oil would be sold before anyone disembarked. Each sailor would receive cash on the barrelhead.

How that translates into modern film terms is that the producer negotiates the distribution deal such that *a specified percentage of the* very first dollar *earned from every sale and/or rental is paid to the producer. And a specified percentage of that is paid to you.* Sign a deal like this and you will see money.

If the distribution deal is "tiered," that is if anybody gets paid any money *before* you, chances are you will never see a penny. Got that? You get a piece of the very first dollar? You'll see money. You don't? You're probably working for love.

The Best *Possible* Deal

Don't let the negotiating spiral out of control. These people are negotiating for and about you. It's your thing. Don't let them harm you and your career by getting into the pissing contests agents, producers, and lawyers sometimes do. Remember that production was delayed for weeks on *The*

Last Temptation of Christ because the lawyers couldn't agree on the sequel rights....

"You got the job!"

The coolest thing you'll ever
hear your agent say.

Seize this moment. Celebrate it. You have just accomplished something that presidents, popes, rocks stars dream of. *You've been hired to direct.*

The moment is perfection. It could easily be one of the key events of your life. It may be your first job. It may be your last. So savor this moment. Because you're about to enter a whole new ball game. You're about to commence the phase of production that dictates how *all* else will go. This set of tasks will set you and the show up for possible success if you do them well but almost certain failure if you don't. I speak of preproduction. Prep.

Shooting from the camera car
Kharen Hill Photo

chapter THREE

PREPRODUCTION

"Be prepared"

Boy Scouts of America motto

Right now you have a few thousand words on paper and a deal memo. But within a very short period of time you will step onto a set with a cast, crew, production equipment, props, locations, and a plan. Where do these elements come from? How did they get here? Preproduction. Prep.

Virtually every single decision regarding the resources you're going to have to tell this story is made during prep. Technically, prep begins when a project is "green lit" (green as in *money* flows) and ends on the first day of principal photography. For the working director, however, prep begins before prep begins.

TOOLS OF THE TRADE
It's worth mentioning at this point that there are some tools you're going to need.

Besides the computer you need in your home and office, a palmtop with fast wireless internet is extremely useful.

A cell phone is indispensable. I do all my studio/network calls from the car riding to and from set. So when I get home at night I get an extra hour or so of r&r.

A digital still camera is invaluable for pitching locations or props to distant producers. It also helps you communicate with your crew during prep.

A GPS unit can be handy for finding set. A satellite phone works great on mountain tops. There's talk of video-like monitors implanted on one's eyeball....

This Sort of Thing is My Bag, Baby

I toss a big old sports bag in my trunk before driving to the production office every day during prep and then take it to set once we're shooting. Everyone has a different list of contents. Here's mine.

Director's Viewfinder
Tina Schliessler Photo

— A director's viewfinder. An actual steel and glass optical device. Mine is small. It telescopes into lens sizes and has inserts for various aspect ratios.

— Rain gear including boots. I buy the best I can afford.

— In winter, warm gear including silk long underwear, polar fleece vests, hand and feet warmers and boots. Again, quality is critical.

— A hat is a must for sun and rain.

— Sun glasses. I use expensive polarized ones. I frequently twist them around to judge if a polarizing filter would get rid of a particular reflection.

— A pad, pen, water, a hundred dollar bill, antacid pills, pain killers, a hairbrush, a small first aid kit, a Frisbee. You'll find yourself in the weirdest situations. It's best to be prepared for anything.

By now it must be fairly obvious that film crew people tend to be gadget people. Some of it you need, some is nice, some is silly. You can waste a lot of time fooling with tech. The whole concept is to save your very limited time.

THE PRODUCTION OFFICE
One of the first calls you're going to receive will be someone from the production office wanting to talk over your schedule for the next few days. On a long form it could be the production coordinator or the producer's assistant calling. On episodic it's always the first assistant director. They'll ask for your contact details, cell phone, fax number. They'll also arrange transportation (if they're driving you) to the production office for the first day of meetings.

If you're working for a studio you'll pull up at the gates, clear security, park, and enter. If your show is an independent you'll pull up at a grungy-looking warehouse with a commercial real estate sign out front. Yes, this is the place. Independent productions rarely waste money on fancy digs. The choice of production office is driven by available space, cheapness of rent, proximity to shooting locations, issues of traffic, crew commute, and so forth.

Follow the signs. Enter the main office. Usually there are two or three workers in the center of a hub of offices. You can expect that the office doors close by will be the producer's, the PM's, the production coordinator's, perhaps the writer's, certainly accounting, and yours. The crafts are usually housed closer to the work spaces. The assistant directors (ADs), the art department, costumes, transportation, and various others depending on the show. There will be a central boardroom for all the meetings. And washrooms and a kitchen/craft service area.

The three or so desk workers are usually very pleasant. They are office production assistants (PAs), maybe an assistant coordinator, possibly an assistant to the producer (who always likes to know who's phoning, who's stopping by). It's their job to run the phones, copy the scripts, distribute the enormous volume of office memos, schedules, etc. They will also usually have a familiarity with the schedule itself. They'll know where everyone is at any given time. And they almost always have valuable insights into the inner workings of the production. Foreign financing falling through? Guess who answers the phone when it's a screaming Spaniard? Star's agent being difficult? Guess who's the first to know? Be nice to the office staff. They work long hours for not great pay. Make them know they're a valued part of your team and you'll be surprised how much they will help you.

And This Will Be Your Office...

Your own personal office is usually subject to directors guild basic agreements. But generally it needs to be big enough to comfortably seat four to six people for all the meetings you'll hold here. You'll need a desk, chairs, a phone, a computer with internet access, a small printer, and various office supplies. There should be a wall you can pin cast photos to. Your office should be private, not shared, with a closable door. Some nice extra touches are a couch, a view, a window that opens, non-fluorescent lights. But don't be too fussy. You won't spend all that much time here.

So you're in your office. You straighten your pens. What next?

First Things First

Your first real order of business is to take the pulse of the place. Is everything good? Is there trouble? Who is the office heavy? Where are the land mines? You need to find someone who knows the ropes, what's what, who's who, what's in the wind. Keep in mind that there is almost always something going on that you should know about. Maybe one of the distributors is fighting with the producer over a certain key cast member. Maybe you're about to unwittingly weigh in on the opposite side from a person you're going to have to work closely with. Find out what's moving under the surface and don't start out on the wrong side of it. In episodic TV the person you'll get the skinny from is almost always your 1st AD. On long forms your guide may be the producer, maybe the coordinator, maybe (but less often) the PM. If at all possible you should make this your first real meeting. Your question to them: *"So, is there anything going on I should know about?"*

One note of caution: Everyone on a show has their own canoe to paddle. Make certain that the picture your guide is painting is not simply their paranoid view of what you would otherwise find to be a trouble-free world.

Natural Friends: There are people in the production office who will find it very much in their interest to get along with you. Principally the director of photography (DP), the designer, your assistant directors (ADs), and most of the keys. Their job is just so much more difficult if you don't share a consensus. Which is not to say that all of these people don't have their own agendas as well. But more on that in a minute.

Natural Enemies: The Godfather, Don Corleone, tells Michael that the one who will betray him will be the one who asks him for a meeting after the Don's death. When you're prepping a movie, if trouble is going to start at this stage the director's very own Clamenza or Tessio will either be the line producer/production manager (PM) or the writer. Why? It's simple. The line producer and the PM are there to deliver the show on (or below) budget. You are there to deliver a great show. Occasionally those two aims can clash. The writer fears you are going to change her words and destroy her vision. Which is not to say there aren't a lot of line producers, PMs, and writers who are mature, honest filmmakers you'll love working with. But this is where the threat seems to come from most often.

There's a simple way to recognize whether these people are enemies or not. It's in how they come at you: straight or manipulative. Straight is when you say: *"I need five helicopter days."* And they say: *"Gee, we only have budget for three. But there may be some fat in locations. Let's see if we can work it out."* If they're prepared to be straight with you, they are not your enemy at all.

But sometimes when you say, *"I need five helicopter days,"* they say, *"WHAT¿¿¿!! Are you crazy!¿ I got budget for a Cessna 172 for half a day, tops!"* They expect you to scream back and ultimately settle for three helicopter days. Because they're certain that's what you really wanted all along.

You need to figure this one out right away. If you are straight with someone like this they'll misinterpret that as your (weak) opening negotiating position and they'll proceed to take away stuff you really need to make the picture. And if you then stick to your guns (thus denying them the opportunity to "beat you down") they'll tell the world you're difficult.

Writers can be like that too. Most are straight. They love writing and problem solving. They know you'll find ways of getting their story to translate from their page to your screen. But some writers have been abused so badly that they take up an extreme defensive position right out of the gate. I recently worked with a writer who adopted this "strategy." In one of our early story conferences I had quite a number of very minor notes. Small dialogue things mostly. I also had five more substantial notes. Things like, *"There's a logical conflict if this character knows something they haven't found out yet."* That sort of thing. The writer fought tooth and nail over every single minor point. No matter how trivial. When it came to the five more important notes he flat out refused to consider changing anything. When I said something about his inflexibility he screamed at me, *"I gave you twelve out of twenty on your list! Who's being inflexible¿!"* That was our last conversation. I got the changes I needed from the producer. Life (and prep) is too short.

THE CONCEPT MEETING

One of your first scheduled meetings will be what is often referred to as the Concept meeting. It is here where you will meet the other department heads (keys) already on the payroll. This is where you will have your first chance to begin to communicate your ideas to some of the people who will help you realize them. It gives the beginnings of your crew their first chance to get a sense of your vision. Which is one of the reasons why your first "who's doing what to who" meeting is so important. If your vision includes that fleet of helicopters, the Concept meeting is an embarrassingly public place to discover that the PM claims to have budget for just one Cessna.

The Concept meeting sets the early priorities. What you can and should expect to come out of it are decisions like, *"We need to find a location that works for both the castle and the pool hall."* Or, *"We need to plan on building the castle interiors on the stage."* Very general big picture stuff.

The Concept meeting is also your chance to demonstrate your tone. They're watching you. They want to know if you're professional, a terminal nice guy, a pushover, a fighter. You are watching the crowd for signs of same.

Meet the Keys

Next will be a series of meetings with the key department heads as they come on board. Here's a place where web access in your office is so handy. *Imdb.com* everyone. Find something you admire in their work and be ready to praise it when you meet them. This sounds phony. And if you're telling them lies about shows you haven't seen then yes, it is phony. So be real. Even *Survivor* has some nice locations work.

In the keys meetings, whether it's for picture cars, makeup, wardrobe, or whatever, the pattern rarely varies. These people have read the script. They have ideas of what their approach should be. They troop into your office with their scripts full of post-its and highlighter marks. What they are looking for is direction from you regarding the elements their department will deliver to you. In the absence of clear ideas from you they want confirmation that *their* ideas are in sync with your vision.

Invariably your opinions and theirs will differ from time to time. That's okay. It's normal. It's not that you differ that's important, it's how you go about it. Done well it can become a rewarding collaboration. Done badly there's a risk they'll dig in their heels.

Take Wardrobe. The costumer has ideas. She'll have magazine cut-outs and perhaps sketches. When she pitches you her ideas she's revealing something personal to you: her taste. Think about it. When your spouse/partner asks your opinion of one of their outfits do you say, *"Nah, looks like crap. What else you got?"* Your spouse/partner may not react well to this. Neither will the costumer. She may take it. She may suffer in silence. You're the director. But she'll find a way to make you pay for your rudeness. She will. How hard would it be to say, *"I see where you're going, interesting. That makes me wonder if perhaps we should consider something a little more like..."* ?

This is another place you'll need your "handle" on the script.

The one you found back when you were first in discussions with the producer. Keys love shorthand. Like you they're busy. If you can tell your DP you were thinking of going with something a bit like a show he knows (or will be able to rent), you're miles ahead. One thing your keys do not want to see is signs of over-controlling. The makeup people are looking for general comments about degrees and color. Not what brand of base to use.

But at the end of the day it's your choice. And sometimes the disagreement you find yourself in with a key is not about content. It's not about budget. It's not about style. It's about *control*. Don't cave in to an overbearing department head. Unchecked they have the ability to ruin your show.

I Really Want to Direct...

Never forget. Some of these people want your job. They know the director gets money, prestige, and power. They often have no clear sense of how hard you had to work to get here. Or how hard you have to work to stay here. Why not? Because they've been too busy working week in, week out, bringing home a steady pay check at their less competitive craft. They never see the years of sacrifice a struggling director makes turning down paying work as a camera assistant or lamp operator.

But it's hard not to sympathize with the key who wants your job. They sometimes see people handed the director's job based on their achievements as a rock star, DP, producer, nephew. These people are often given directing work without acquiring the skills. Crews are sometimes forced to carry an incompetent or otherwise irrelevant director. The crew people *know* they could direct better. It's a frequent topic of conversation in the lunch line.

Which is why you need to convince them that a) you have earned your job; b) you will pull your weight; and c) it is *in their self interest to work with you.* Make them believe in your talent. Make them realize that you'll be working a lot in the years to come. That you're someone who'll be in a position to *hire them* in the future. Who doesn't want to work with competent people they like and trust?

With a Little Help From My Friends

It's great to hire as many of "your people" as possible for obvious reasons. Generally (although not in episodic) you'll have most say in the hiring of the DP and your 1st AD. Because they're the ones you work closest with. But there's no reason you can't put forward your other friends. It is an absolute joy to build up over time a group of people you love to work with. If someone is capable, honest, enthusiastic, and on your wavelength, it's a real find. And in all honesty most of the people you work with will be this way. The majority of people who work in our business do so because they love it. They love being good at what they do.

THE ASSISTANT DIRECTOR

During prep there's one department you will be working with more than any of the others. The *directing* department. The assistant directors. The ADs.

Put simply, the ADs calculate what elements the director is going to need to tell the story and when they're going to need them. Need actors? The ADs organize their pick-up. They monitor their progress through hair/makeup/wardrobe. They deliver them to set just as the director is ready for them. Need a second unit to shoot sunsets from a downtown skyscraper?

The ADs schedule it. They put it on the call sheet. It's done.

It's easy to see why the ADs are often considered to be part of the line producer/PM's team. They live where the rubber meets the road. If an AD department works well, things go smoothly. If not, the most minor AD mistake can cost a production thousands of dollars. PMs and ADs maintain a constant dialogue.

From your POV the assistant director is there for one primary thing. To provide what you need to tell the story. There is sometimes also a sense of mentorship. Many of the people who work as assistant directors hope to one day move up into the director position. The concept is that by observing closely they'll acquire the tools of the trade. It's been my observation that the more an AD enjoys the filmmaking process, the more they'll resist the pull to side with the line producer. And the more likely that AD will make the transition into directing. Conversely, the more business-oriented an AD is, the more likely they'll transition into line producing.

Directing the Schedule

During prep all the work the ADs do becomes formalized into one document: the **schedule**. From the schedule flows everything: the actors' bookings, special equipment needs, call times, shooting order, everything. The schedule dictates what order you will do things in and what resources you'll have to do them. In prep a smart director is all over the schedule like a tourist at a Vegas buffet.

From the outset it's good to discuss the schedule with the AD in general terms to see that you're on the same page. Comments like, *"Okay, looks like one week in the mountains, two weeks on the main farm, a week on the stage, and a week of second unit. Sound about right?"* Because if you're shooting what you believe to be an action picture and you get handed a schedule with three weeks of studio dialogue and one week of action... you're not shooting an action picture.

What influence can you have on the schedule during prep? Lots.

Want to shoot sequentially (scene 45 before 46)? In many cases it's possible to schedule at least the scenes you shoot on any given day more or less sequentially. Your cast will love you for it and you'll get better performances. Let your AD know and work the schedule with them.

You visit the location and realize the best sunlight position there is in the morning? Work the schedule.

Want to give your cast an early wrap? A long weekend? Work the schedule.

You and your 1st AD can work together like partners. The big thing is communication. Let your AD know what you need. I always give them my general schedule notes right away. I'll tell them I need x amount of time alone in the locations. Usually weekends. I'll want to meet with all the actors prior to the read through (usually a drink at night). I'll want to shoot sequentially wherever possible. On night shoots I'll want to schedule the heavy stuff before lunch (crews get sleepy after eating) and so on. In other words I let the AD know how to schedule me.

But Sometimes...

There will be the odd occasion when you end up with a 1st AD whose personal style conflicts with yours. On a long form show if you can't fix it really fast in prep, talk to the producer. You can live with an unpleasant lamp operator. But you have to spend all day every day with the AD. See about replacing him.

Obviously in episodic TV, unless the AD goes insane and starts coming to work naked he's not going to be replaced. Regardless of how much you may dislike him. So deal with it. Direct him. Be professional. Do your job competently. Don't make dumb mistakes. Maybe even catch the AD in a few errors. Make him stay on his toes. Worst case you'll end up with a professional relationship. And just maybe... sooner or later the AD will realize you're not the enemy.

Charles with AD James Marshall and DP Tobias Schliessler
Kharen Hill Photo

PREPPING THE SCRIPT

Prep is your last real chance to deal with the script as a whole. Once shooting starts you'll be focused on acts, scenes, lines, shots.

Does prepping the script mean changing the script? To one degree or another, yes. And know this: Arguments over changing the script are the number one cause of director/producer friction during prep. To begin with, what exactly is the director's responsibility to the script during prep?

> *The director's duty to the screenplay during prep is to make every reasonable effort to ensure that the final shooting script you take before the camera will allow the writer's ideas to flow smoothly from page to stage such that the best possible film is made.*

Nothing more. Nothing less. Prepping the script is polishing off any rough edges that could impede the *translation* from the writer's written word to the screen. Because that is exactly what the director does with the screenplay – *translate*.

The way a language translator works is to first understand the meaning of the work in the original language. Then they find the ideas/images/words that will express that meaning in the target language. If an American character says, *"I want a hot dog..."* and if the translator translates word for word into French, the result is *"Je veux un chien chaud."* Literally *"I want a canine at high temperature."* In short, gibberish.

Likewise take a screenplay that says:

```
INT. WOODSHED — NIGHT
Susan opens the door and stops.

CUT TO
Her eyes widen.

SMASH CUT TO
The THING lunges at her.

                    SUSAN
           Oh my God!!!
```

Obviously a director is not going to stop filming just before Susan's eyes widen and punch in for a close-up. That's what editors are for. But what happens if the Thing that special FX delivers to set is especially horrifying? What if the actor's *"Oh my God"* is entirely inappropriate? The writer's intent here is fairly clear. The suggestions she's provided with "Cut To" and "Smash Cut To" help the director to understand the writer's *intent*. But does the writer/producer really want the director to obey the script word for word? To blindly present the audience with a canine at high temperature?

Judgment is required during every translation process. That's why computerized translation programs don't work very well. That's why producers hire directors. Otherwise they'd save the salary and get the writer to oversee things. Smart producers working with competent directors know that there are judgment calls in the director's handling of the script.

So in prep what exactly is the director's duty to the script? I'll say it again:

> *The director's duty to the screenplay during prep is to make every reasonable effort to ensure that the final shooting script you take before the camera will allow the writer's ideas to flow smoothly from page to stage such that the best possible film is made.*

What's on the Table?

What should you be asking for? The kinds of changes I frequently ask for in prep have to do with things like awkward dialogue. Or I'll ask for a scene's location to be moved to an exterior if we've found a great location. Or I'll question the logic of what and when a character knows. Translating the writer's intent to the screen.

What shouldn't you be asking for? Well... if it's a bio pic about the life of Mother Theresa, prep is not the place to be arguing for a car chase. You should have raised an issue this fundamental in your first meeting with the producer so they could have found someone else.

Approaching Change

You'll recall that when you first read the script you gave the producer notes. Possibly ones that the writer has by now addressed. At that time you may have been less critical when you were trying to land the job than you are now when you're faced with actually doing the job. If so this is where you'll have to deal with the consequences.

As the director, there are three basic situations you can find yourself in at this stage:

1. You have a great script — no changes are needed.

2. You have a good script — it needs minor cosmetic work.

3. You have a weak script with major structural problems.

Let's talk only about the most common case, #2. After all, if your script is terrific there's little to talk about. And if it's awful you need to first find out if the producer's *primary* goal is to make a good show. And if so get a good writer and get to work.

So you have a good script and you want to get it ready for shooting. How to proceed in these shark infested waters?

Re-Re-Read the Script

As many times in as many ways as you can. Read it considering *time passage*. Frequently you'll find that one day seems impossibly long and you'll want to consider putting a night in between. This is usually the result of a lot of scene juggling by the writer.

Read the script from each character's point of view. Sometimes one character winds up with someone else's lines. Another computer editing glitch.

Read looking for legitimate prep issues. Things that need to be changed because of changes that have arisen in prep. You've cast a formerly male role with a female actor? You may need dialogue changes. You've decided to shoot a scene interior instead of exterior? The script needs to say that or the various departments won't know.

Read looking for any logic gaps. Places where you suddenly see things that don't make sense. Characters who know things they couldn't possibly know. Or who act as though they've seen or heard something we know they haven't. Like the "too long day" syndrome these types of mistakes frequently occur as a result of the extensive cutting and pasting writers often do.

Read looking for dialogue inconsistencies and just plain awkward or uncommunicative lines. If you don't your actors will. And remind your producer that it's way less expensive re-writing dialogue during prep than on set.

Read looking for weak or missing devices. The easiest way to sniff out an ineffective device is to look for scenes that are in and of themselves not very entertaining but are there to establish this or that important fact for later on. A good device shouldn't need to be propped up by bad ones. Challenge the writer to find a more direct way.

Read looking for genre conflicts. Many people who saw the remarkable *What Dreams May Come* loved its amazingly positive depiction of heaven but thought the intensely Catholic depiction of hell was from a different movie, even a different genre. Clearly the film was targeting the New Age audience, a group that generally rejects the old-fashioned, vengeful depiction of hell. It's arguable that the picture may have found an even wider audience if the Robin Williams walking over upturned, protesting grey dead faces scene had found its way onto the director's "different movie" list.

Big List Small List

Got your list? Cut it in two: 1) Things you can shoot around or otherwise deal with yourself; and 2) Things that must be addressed by the writer/producer. Because you need to consider how large a problem you're about to become. The total size of your list is critical. Walk into this conversation with a long list, even if most of your points are trivial things caused by casting and location issues and there's a real danger you'll get a percentage of what you need and then they'll start digging in.

With each point ask yourself: Do I need this changed in the script? Or can I as the director deal with it in shooting? Anything you can shoot around or cut around, don't bother them with it.

Of the things you can't do yourself, logic gaps are fairly easy to raise. Usually a writer will see the light. Time problems ditto. Dialogue is tougher. If they resist, you have to accept that you'll find some way of making the actor say it. But you can always plan to shoot with lots of coverage so you can remove the offensive dialogue in your cut.

Weak devices are sometimes real sticking points. A writer will live with these things so long they forget what they're for. If the writer/producer resists, ask yourself if you can shoot it to make it clear. If not, here's a place you may need to stand and fight. Remember, if the script is asking you to shoot uninteresting scenes just to prop up an important point then the device isn't working.

Having separated the things you as director can fix from the things you need help with, it's time to cut your "need help" list in two again. Cut it into simple stuff and bigger stuff.

Take both lists into the writer/producer meeting. Start small. See how it goes. If your minor ideas are met with professionalism, graduate to larger ones. If you meet "over my dead body" kind of resistance, either forget about your major list or reconsider the style of your approach.

Earn the Right To Change

A director has to *earn* the trust of the writer and producer. That trust doesn't come automatically with signing a deal memo. Ask yourself, if I were Martin Scorsese would they listen to my script notes? In a heartbeat they would. So maybe the problem isn't your ideas. Maybe it's you. It's the old adage: "If you're so smart, how come you ain't famous?" That's hard to argue with. By all means give the producer the chance to look at your ideas. But if you ain't famous what makes your judgment better than theirs? Bottom line — they own the project. They hired you. If they're telling you the script is finished prepping... the script is finished prepping. Move on.

What's next? On all shows except ones shot entirely on a stage, it's time to get into the van.

THE LOCATION SCOUT
Everyone knows that most films and TV shows shoot at a combination of specially built sets in a studio and out on locations. "Location" is any place where filming takes place away from the studio or sound stage. A house, a stadium, an airport, whatever.

The primary challenge with location scouting is to find as many excellent locations as possible at as few actual venues as possible, the goal being *to have the least number of unit moves*. Whether your production unit is a few cars or dozens of giant production trucks, moving is time consuming and expensive. If you can shoot in one location for at least an entire day the transport folks can move during the night. Even then their overtime is expensive and your crew takes time settling into every new location. As the director, time spent moving is *lost time*. Lost time translates into lost shots, lost set-ups, lost chances for brilliant performances.

There is also the cost consideration. Some locations are outrageously expensive. Some are free. Some cost a lot to control traffic or pedestrians. Some are empty. Some you can drive to. Some you can't even chopper in. All these factors impact on the budget and the schedule.

Location selection and planning takes up a big chunk of prep. The shooting schedule you and the ADs are working on is very much dependent upon which scene will be shot at what location. Say your script calls for a mansion location as well as fields, a swimming pool, and a garage. If you find a country manor location that has excellent sites for all of these things you will obviously schedule the shooting of the mansion scenes back to back with the fields, pool, and garage scenes. If on the other hand the manor has no pool and the only suitable one is miles away you will schedule that for a different day. Maybe even a different week. Which is going to have an impact on the dates you schedule your actors for. Which could have an impact on one or more actor's availability. It's all interconnected. So the sooner you get a range of excellent choices for your locations, the sooner your schedule will start becoming real.

The way the process will begin is this: After the concept

meeting the AD will schedule a meeting between you and the Location Manager (LM) who will by now have a sense of what you're looking for. The LM will have pulled or created a series of file folders full of photos of more or less appropriate locations. Your interest will be aroused to a greater or lesser degree. You'll need a closer look. The AD will schedule a location scout.

Does the working director need to prep for a location scout? Very much so.

The Location Script Breakdown

When the LM shows you a potential location, you need to know what's being proposed that you could shoot there. Kitchen scene? Garden? How many pages? Day? Night? Without this knowledge at your fingertips, how can you assess the potential of a given spot?

I carry this info with me in my palmtop computer. It's a simple location script breakdown which I will have by now either got from the ADs or have done myself. The breakdown lists how many pages I will be shooting in each location. I will have a summary page that ranks the locations on a pages per basis. In this manner I can tell at a glance where I'll be spending the most time shooting. Now I can prioritize the relative importance of a given location. There are numerous cases that defy this type of classification. "The Indians take the fort" is a classic example of a scene that will take far longer to shoot than its one-line description would otherwise rate. But there's nothing stopping me from placing this scene at the top of my priority list. It's my list.

So if we're scouting that mansion location I have at my fingertips that we will be shooting:

Kitchen: *10 pages*
Stables: *8 3/8 pages*
Gardens: *4 2/8 pages*
Entry: *1 6/8 pages*

This makes it easy to see what the priorities are. If I don't do this, someone on the location scout could fall in love with a great entry room where we're only shooting one page and I'll be under pressure to accept an otherwise poor location for that one minor point.

I will also have generated in my palmtop a list of scenes — *by location* — with a short description of each. It reads like this:

Kitchen Scenes:

Scn 25. 3 pgs. Joe and Sue enter, prepare hot knish on counter top

Scn 37. 4 pgs. Joe talks on phone to Emma, Sue enters, chases w/sword

Scn 85. 2 pgs. Police question Sue at table, forensics photograph Joe

This way when we're on the location scout, while the other crew people are walking around making comments like *"Nice room,"* I can direct the group to assess the potential of the room in concrete script terms. *Joe goes here. Sue exits there.*

Who Sits Where

On a location scout the director sits in the front seat of the van beside the driver. It's partly a convention. A respect thing. It's also a visibility thing. You can see better in the front seat. Some directors make a big thing of it. I often find that I can get more done with the keys in the back seat. When I'm in the front I always end up with a stiff neck from turning around. Generally on the early scouts I'll take the front seat. We don't have that much to talk about yet. Later when it's just the LM, the DP, the designer and I, we can sit together and work.

Who Is Pitching You What?

When the van pulls up at a potential location everybody gets out to look. As director you're looking for a great backdrop for the actors and wonderful places that will bring your story to life. You assume that is everyone's top priority as well. But it often isn't. So what is everybody else looking for?

The LM is looking for crew parking, unit parking, space for craft service, space for the caterers, the lunch tent, extras holding. She's also looking for potential neighbor problems, noise issues, shooting curfews. And of course, expense. The LM has a budget like every department.

The AD is looking for bogies. Is there an airport close by? Is the traffic hard to control? We lose shooting time waiting for sound. Do we have a long shuttle from the unit to set? We lose time shuttling the crew back and forth at lunch. Is the location sensitive? Does the crew have to wear booties to protect the floors? We lose time. Are the rooms small? Will the crew be bumping into each other? We lose time.

The PM is looking for all of the above. Plus, he's assessing how tough it's going to be to move his people and gear over the terrain, up and down stairs. He's measuring how much cable needs to be laid. How many lights, cranes, etc. Because all this costs money. Money that won't appear on the screen. Money he won't have for your crane or your Steadicam. When the PM says, *"Hey, this is great..."* most times it will mean, *"Hey, this place works for the show."* But sometimes it will mean, *"Hey, this place works for the budget."* And sometimes you'll wonder what he's been smoking.

Even the designer is not necessarily focused on your goals. She wants a look that will fit into her vision for the show. She doesn't have to worry about moving actors through the set.

You the director have to build a solid wall between your right and left brains. You need to be able to build a door through that wall that you can slam and lock. When you are on the right side there's only one question: Does shooting my movie here help or hinder the telling of this story? When you're on the left side you're asking: What practical considerations could help or hinder my telling of the story in this place?

Once you get out of the van you need to move fast. Opinions are being formed. First impressions sometimes crystallize into production decisions with dizzying speed. Location scouting is like shoe shopping. Some people take forever. Others are in and out of the store in a heartbeat. The only way to keep the high ground here is to be better prepared than anyone else and get in there first.

Walk Right In

I enter a given space knowing that the LM is showing it to me as the kitchen or dining room or whatever. But I remain open to considering the place as something else as well. The first thing I look for is the "album cover." The one angle that visually communicates what we're going to pretend this place is. If I'm making a scary thriller on a farm I want to be able to put my viewfinder to my eye and see a really scary-looking farm house. Or at least one that can be made to look so within our budget. There has to be a background for a great shot here. Otherwise why are we looking at it? Okay, the parking may be great. The parking is great at WalMart too. The location has to communicate.

Once I'm standing in front of that spot I imagine the scene. I raise my viewfinder and rapidly visualize the action we'd be staging here. How does it work? Is there a beautiful shot? Is it too small, too big, too ugly?

I always shoot digital pictures of the potential locations. I try to frame and compose to reflect the actual shots I'll be shooting there. These photos are valuable for selling a location to a producer and for communication with the keys.

I often ask someone on the scout to stand in for me, a human body to help the framing. I will often maintain a running commentary: *"So, we have the couple arguing here. She gets up and moves to this exit. He remains with us. We're shoot-ing over his shoulder. Hmm."* Or *"Gee, shooting into a corner here. Not much of a view there. Kinda tight here. No room for the dolly track. Hmm."*

I point out the deficiencies from my point of view. If it's too small to shoot in I say so right away. Ditto if it's uncinematic. I try to avoid big arguments at this point but if someone really starts pushing for an unworkable location I'll usually play devil's advocate. I'll try and stage the scene right on the spot. Five times out of ten it becomes obvious to everyone why it won't work. The other five times I learn something.

And my eyes are always open to what else we can shoot there. What other scenes. Fewer moves = more movie.

It's a good general policy not to wax overly enthusiastic or pessimistic at this stage. If I know the LM has other choices I ask to see them before I express a strong preference.

It's not my job to comment on the unit parking or the flights of stairs the gear needs to go up. I generally notice that stuff but only use it if I need ammo to shoot down a bad location being pushed on me.

The Decision

The final decision as to where you shoot will be made based on a whole range of questions. It's a constant juggling act between aesthetics, cost, and schedule.

Usually there's give and take. Sometimes the best location is just not affordable. That's where horse trading comes in. If it's between great and good, consider being flexible. But if it's between great and terrible, fight the fight. Don't over-compromise. After all, Mona Lisa framed against a background of a fifteenth-century Italian stockyard just wouldn't be the same.

CASTING

Prep is now well under way. Many pots are simmering. Some on the back burner. Some beginning to boil. Yes, the DP is putting together a list of special lenses and mounts you might need. But you can deal with that any time up to a few days before shooting. The one issue you need to be on top of from early in prep is casting.

Non insiders imagine casting to be one of the really great things about the director's job. Popular culture has it that the director casts his or her eye over the available field. He does a few lunches, perhaps considers making one young hopeful or another into a star. He accepts or rejects the plentiful casting couch invitations and finally nods this way or that. And it's suddenly all over E-Tonight. It may be that's the producer's experience of casting. But the majority of working directors often don't play much of a role in the star search.

So Where Do the Stars Come From?

On virtually all commercial films and TV shows the stars are part of the financing package. An example: a producer pitches a show. The Studio/Network/Distributor says, *"Get a star from this list, you got a deal."* So on most shows the star cast is in place before the director is hired. That process frequently doesn't involve much or any involvement from the director. Are there exceptions? Sure. Do you personally know an approvable star on one of the lists who'll do the show? Great. Call the casting director. Put the name forward. Let them know you have a relationship. If your choice is cast you get an actor who's right for the part. Someone who knows they're there because you want them to be. Win/win. But supposing you don't know a listed star. You can still play but it's a lot more difficult.

Every year there's a piece of brilliant casting that takes the audience by storm. When Mickey Rooney came out of virtual retirement to do *Black Stallion,* scores of lapsed movie goers came out and bought tickets to see an old friend. Art Carney in *Harry and Tonto,* Madonna in *Desperately Seeking Susan,* Martin Sheen in *The West Wing,* Bill Murray in *Lost in Translation,* Charlton Heston in *Bowling For Columbine* — brilliant casting. None of these picks were obvious at the time. All of them were someone's great idea. There's no reason the next great idea can't be yours.

Wrack your brains. Spend time cruising old movie shelves. Open a line of dialogue with your casting director. Cast your movie.

And Featuring...

Working directors generally have much more involvement in casting the non-starring roles. Most directors who have worked for any length of time have a group of favorite actors they like to cast regularly. The time to put those names forward is now, when you have your first phone conversation with the casting director. Be prepared. The casting director is in the midst of organizing a casting session for the actors auditioning for the smaller roles. Tell the casting director who you want to put up for consideration. They'll bring them in. Likewise if there are actors you'd like to see read with other actors, now's the time to ask for them.

The casting director will very likely know the actors you're asking for and will usually be happy to bring them in. But if you snooze you may very well lose. If the first casting session goes without your picks you may never get another chance.

The Casting Session

Seasoned directors have cast many times. You may want to skip ahead. For the rest here's an important note: Be on time. The schedule is often tight: ten to fifteen minutes per actor. You can create a real backlog by being only a few minutes late.

You will usually be sitting at a table. The assistant casting director will give you the session list and offer you coffee.

A video camera will be set up to record the session for the executives who can't be there. And there's a monitor so you can watch how the actors photograph. Attending will usually be the director, the casting director, their assistants, someone to organize the arriving actors, and often one or more producers.

The first actor will be called in. She hands you her head shot and resume. She often wants to shake hands. I don't much care either way but some producers are concerned about germs and it can be sort of embarrassing. Establish a policy and try to stick to it, *"Hi, we're not shaking"* sort of thing. If the actor hasn't read the entire script, a few comments from you regarding who/what/where the character is can be helpful. The assistant rolls tape. They have already slated or the actor does, *"Hi, Janyne D'eau from Thespians R Us Talent, I'm reading for Blanche."* The assistant designated to read off-camera lines stands beside the camera to keep the eye line close. She reads the scene partner's dialogue. Away they go.

Watch the screen. Watch the actor. Listen. You're at a play, watching a performance. When she's finished, if she shows some potential ask for it again. Give her some simple direction, *"Try and internalize your pain, show me less but feel it more."* That sort of thing will show if she's flexible and directable.

This is one of my favorite parts of the whole business. It's like picking up a new instrument to see how it plays. When the actor has finished I try to find something positive and real to say about what he's offered up. I thank him and he leaves. After he's gone I always ask for one or two minutes to write down my reactions. I'll often compare him to a known actor. Things like, *"Matt Dillon-like. Not 100% but maybe."* Otherwise after we've auditioned twenty or thirty actors they can start to blur.

Frequently when someone reads for one part they'll seem better for another. Ask the casting director to have him wait outside. Confer, then the casting director can tell the actor what's going on and ask if he'd like to cold read or come back when we're doing call-backs. It's worth mentioning that frequently no one will be right for a particular role but when you study your notes and the tape later you'll find the perfect choice in someone who read for a different role.

I try really hard to separate my personal response to the person from my calculated appraisal of his performance. All the audience ever sees is how the actor performs on the screen in this role. It matters not at all that he can chat cleverly to the director about whatever.

That being said I also try really hard to be kind and have fun with them. I love actors. They put everything on the line. Of course they're disappointed if they don't get the job. So am I. But deep down we both know that casting is a quest for the perfect match between actor and role. And if someone is miscast who's it going to help? Taken this way casting can be a joy.

Call-backs

It's rare to get everybody cast in one session. Perhaps the producers are elsewhere. Or some of the possible choices are on demo tape. You may need to see specific actors acting together. Or you're simply not sure. You do call-backs. Don't worry too much about inconveniencing the actors. The second best thing actors can tell their friends is that they got a call-back.

When the session is over it's not unusual to discuss your reactions and picks. Frequently there's very little disagreement over most of the roles. It's often that obvious.

MEET THE STARS

When the star of the show is more important to the financing than the director it can have a real impact on the star/director relationship.

But look at it another way. *Top* stars have director approval. Top stars all want to work with the director *du jour*. But in this case, they're working with *you*. Whatever the reason, this is a tremendous compliment.

Three Things Stars Want From Directors

1. Are you going to direct a film they will be proud of?

2. Can they trust you? Do you know what you're doing? Or is listening to you going to make them look really stupid?

3. Is the film you're making going to enhance or detract from their industry stature/commercial value?

Three Things Directors Want From Stars

1. Are they or can they become right for the part?

2. Are they prepared to trust me?

3. Are they here to do good work or are they just paying the bills?

How Do You Find Out?

Although this discussion is aimed at directors the ideas are equally useful to actors.

Rent their previous shows. Call other directors who have worked with this particular actor. As soon as she's officially been cast, ask the casting director to get her number from her agent. Call her up. Now that you've become familiar with her work you won't have any trouble telling her how excited and honored you are to be working with her. This isn't too early to ask if she's concerned about anything. Give her your numbers. Tell her to call night or day. Set up a face to face meeting. Something really informal is often best, like a coffee or a drink.

Getting To Know You

I always find the first moment huge when I meet the person who is to be the star of my show. You know what he looks like and acts like on screen. But what is he "really" like?

The conversation will probably start with light stuff. You're both trying to get a sense of who the other is and why you're doing this. Both of you are in it for the art, the money, or some of each. How much of each is the question you're both here to find out.

It's great to get the conversation headed toward each of your respective points of view on the project. If the star feels the comedy you're directing is a dark tragedy, now would be a real good time to find that out.

In the first informal meeting it's worth asking your star what style of shooting he feels comfortable with. Long complex masters or cut up coverage. Find out if he has a bad side to his face (many actors do) so you can plan the coverage accordingly. Likewise it's good to know if he wants his close-up first or last. It's worth telling him about your style and any unusual practices you might have. Lots of rehearsal, 2nd camera, etc.

By the same token I try to tell the star some of my concerns. Like if the show is badly pressed for time. Or if there are ongoing script concerns that performance could help. Or if there's potential personnel problems (a difficult actor or producer).

I also attempt to give the star a quick way to read me. I'll tell him that I'm not a game player. I never have a secret agenda. I'm not a shouter (so don't wait for me to shout to know you're getting to me). And I won't ask for stuff I don't need. If on a rare occasion on set I say to the star, *"We're falling way behind, I need to do this one quickly and simply so we can spend time on the complicated stuff later,"* then I really mean it.

Finally (and I appreciate it's lousy poker) I always let the star know that I know they *are* the show. I let them know I'll do anything in my power to create and protect a bubble around them within which they can feel safe and creative *and breathe their life into this story.*

Melissa Gilbert and Charles filming ABC-TV Seduction
Tina Schliessler Photo

The Many Others

Directors should have actor friends. They should talk to them. Know what the actors say? *"How come directors don't care about me? They don't call, they often don't talk to me on set. What's with that?"* I call every single actor who's cast in a show of mine regardless of the size of their role. It's amazing how much rainy night, overtime, freezing my ass off but have to perform goodwill can be created with a simple welcome aboard and thanks so much for joining our adventure.

LOCATION PLANNING

By now we're well into prep. Casting is falling into place. The script is evolving nicely. Locations are being confirmed. Next step? I ask my AD to book me a series of mornings or afternoons or weekends to visit the confirmed locations alone. I take my script, palmtop, cell phone, viewfinder, a comfortable chair, and if it's remote, something for lunch.

I enter a location, set up my chair, boot my palmtop, open the script, read the first scene and... wait.

I'm waiting to see the scene come to life before my eyes. Sometimes it takes an hour of re-reading, pacing the room, looking through the viewfinder from every angle. Sometimes I take large cut-out characters to people the scene with. What am I looking for?

The Master

I spend a good 80% of my time during location planning coming up with an interesting master shot for each scene. A master can be defined as follows:

> *The master shot is one continuous take that begins at the start of an entire or partial scene, ends at the end, and cinematically tells the entire story of the scene. Preferably without the need of any supporting coverage shots.*

A good master has movement, rhythm, pace. It allows the cast to really act out and refine the scene before commencing the often confusing work of close-ups. By manipulating camera position and actor blocking a good master alternates between wide view and close-up. It is therefore very cuttable.

It makes excellent use of the outstanding features of the location. And most importantly, it tells the story.

I read the scene. I then look for what's best in the location. What view tells the story of this location? What brought me here? It never ceases to amaze me how often emerging directors squander their location for no good reason. They'll read in the script that a foursome sits around a table after dinner drinking wine and talking. They'll walk into a location with a poor dining room but a fabulous living room. They'll create a shot looking into a corner with no room to move and nowhere to light from. When I mention that four-somes often drink wine sitting in a living room (not unlike this fabulous one right here, for example), I almost always get back, *"But the script says a dining room table."*

Or they'll start their shot looking at the interesting background but have their actors walk into a corner where they'll play the scene against a wall. I have been taught to find the best background and set the bulk of the scene *there*. Then plan backwards to find a good opening frame the actors can pass through on the way to where it's great. Often it's as simple as moving a prop into position to create a good scene opening.

Let's say I'm doing location prep for a scene in a prison cell. I have a choice. I can shoot into the cell. In other words I can set my scene to play against three walls and a toilet I could have built in the studio. (So what am I doing out here on location?) Or I can wander into the back of the cell. I raise my viewfinder. I see that if I shoot this way my background is the central cell block. Layers and layers of cages. Cool.

So I've got my background. The direction the camera will be looking. Now I review the business of the scene. Let's say character X is painting a picture, Y enters, they talk, Y exits. I may look at the idea of starting the scene very close on the painting then track back as Y enters. I may plan for Y to come up behind X and remain behind him such that they are both more or less facing camera. I'll remain in that very interesting two shot as they chat. Then I'll pan over and push in close on X for a scene end. I try it with my viewfinder and my cut-outs. I look to see that there's room for the dolly. There's a simple, elegant master. I'll consider whether I want to try for close-ups as well if that fits the visual style. That's my scene.

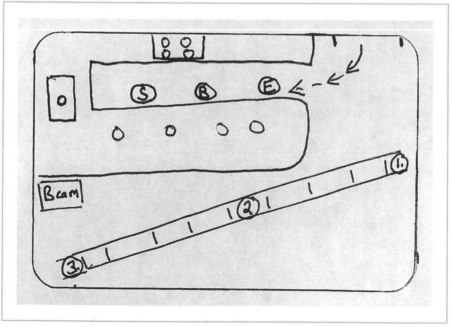

Simple Plot Plan noting actor, track, and camera positions

Next I'll sketch a simple *plot plan* of the location into my palmtop. I copy that plan for as many scenes as I have on that particular set. Then for each scene I note dolly track location. I note 1st, 2nd, 3rd camera positions, actor positions, and so forth. In the database part of this file I'll note shot details, actor action, coverage plans, lens selections, etc. This is the key document that will provide most of the information I need to create my daily shot list.

On this plot plan I will also sketch in the precise location of all movable decoration, furniture etc. I make certain the art department gets a copy so when I arrive on the shooting day the actors are walking where they should because I had set dec put the furniture where I wanted it to be. If I don't do this I'll arrive on set on the day and the actors will block around the furniture the way set dec wants. In other words the set decorator is directing my scene.

Now I photograph my location angles with the digital camera and make whatever notes I need to discuss with my keys. Planning this precisely reveals particular needs. Perhaps I'll realize that we could use a neon sign for the dispensary over there, memo the art dept. I'll see we could use a lot more extras in the background, memo the AD. I'll see the walls are too close, memo camera dept for a wider angle. I'll see the armed guard stations in the corners, the actor should note them in his dialogue. Memo the writer. Memo the armorer.

I depart the location when I know pretty much what I'm going to do there. I've got enough info now to direct every department affected by my discoveries and my plans.

Old school palmtop with scene plan
Tina Schliessler Photo

STORYBOARD?

Some directors storyboard everything. If it helps them visualize, great. In my experience the crew rarely looks at that stuff. Storyboards of wide shots and close-ups of people talking are not all that riveting. One place storyboarding is very useful is in planning action scenes with a lot of coverage. Another is for effects-laden scenes.

There are two basic styles of storyboard: comic strip and shot list. Most storyboard artists favor the comic strip style. This is where the story flows from one panel to another, cutting from wide shot to close-up to insert in the linear manner a comic book does. These boards are fun to read and they get their creator compliments. But unless there's a need to introduce and sell a new and complex sequence and unless the director works closely with the artist it's just a waste of time. It gives an unacceptable degree of directorial control to a storyboard artist.

Here's a situation where the comic strip style worked well for me. I was doing an action picture with a scripted scene that had our heroine climbing from one apartment balcony to the next evading a killer. The location we had was a beautiful old downtown hotel with a green copper roof — but no balconies. I was location planning alone up on the roof deck. I read and re-read the scene. I finally realized that the story beat was simply that we get the character to escape death in some cinematic way. I thought, *why not have her slide down the roof?* This was a 20-story building.

I made some notes. I drew some boards. I went to the producer. His response to my verbal pitch: *"No way, far too expensive. How we gonna do that?"* I showed him my storyboards. The boards made it clear that a very exciting scene could be created very simply and inexpensively. Five minutes later he was booking the stunt doubles and ordering up the special rigs. It was a remarkable sequence.

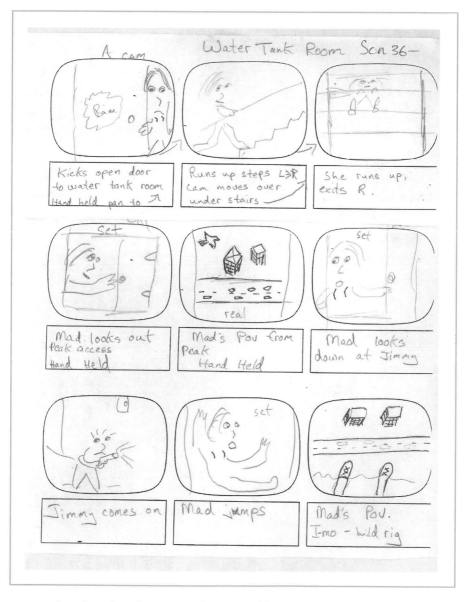

Storyboard roof sequence from Republic Pictures Breach of Trust

Storyboard roof sequence from Republic Pictures Breach of Trust

Storyboard roof sequence from Republic Pictures Breach of Trust

The second type, the **shot list** style of storyboard, is used to explain the director's intentions for an already scripted complex action sequence where there's to be a significant contribution from Stunts, FX, Visual FX, and/or maybe 2nd unit. It's important to spell out your intentions to the team.

These boards are what the name implies. They are an illustrated shot list. What I do is draw a stick man frame of the first master shot. If it's a moving shot I'll show first frame, middle, and end. Then I'll draw and list the coverage, the close-ups, inserts, and so forth for that segment of the scene. Then the next master. Then the subsequent coverage. I do them in what I anticipate will be shooting order.

When the boards are done I'll schedule a meeting with Stunts, FX, and/or Vis FX, present them with my plan, and ask them for input. I notice the team tends to get way more creative when there's a coherent plan to work from rather than when we're starting from scratch in a group think. Once the action team has reached a consensus I incorporate changes and issue revised boards. I copy all the affected departments and note the areas that will be affected: props, wardrobe, transport, locations, etc.

An Imperfect Plan

It goes without saying that you'll miss wonderful stuff in prep. You always arrive on set with a less than perfect plan. But in the high pressure of production there's only one thing worse than an imperfect plan — no plan at all.

The location planning I do becomes the shot list I take to set on the day. I present it to the DP as a starting point. The DP will almost always have ideas to enhance mine or completely replace them with something better. Great. Often an actor will suggest a blocking change that's vastly superior. Terrific. While it's fun to inspire in the crew a sense of confidence, I'm not there to be right. I'm the first one to abandon my carefully made plan if something better comes along. But I watch the blocking process carefully. If I sense it's spinning out of control or if we're starting to fall behind, I have a back-up plan. My shot list based on my prep notes.

Saving Time For What?

If I'm making all these production decisions in prep on my own without the expert creative input of my keys what am I doing on set? Isn't that supposed to be the creative crucible of filmmaking? Depends on your POV. Some directors think directing is about where to put the camera. I personally think that's a very small part of the job. Of course a director needs to acquire technical fluency and yes, location planning is mostly about technical considerations. But I believe that *prep* is where the directors put their stamp on the look of the show. If the director preps properly, by the time the shooting schedule commences the DP can take it from there on set.

Which leaves the director free to do what you are there for. To work with the actors. To watch that each of the critical story beats is coming across. To feel the mood of the scene. To sense the pacing, the tone. In short, to tell the story. If you prep right you will carve out for yourself the calm detachment that on-set creativity depends on.

The Night Before

Prep ends. Usually much too soon. But ready or not the evening will come when you set your alarm clock and turn in for one last good sleep before the madness of production commences. Tomorrow is the first day of shooting.

Sweet dreams.

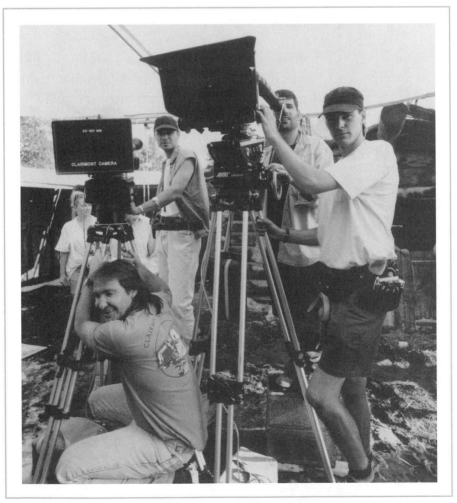

A & B cameras ready to shoot.
Kharen Hill Photo

chapter FOUR

SHOOTING

"We shot a feature all morning, a TV movie all afternoon, and Reality TV for the last hour of O.T."

Common film set complaint

A typical working director's day begins hours before call. If set (shooting) call is at 7 a.m., and crew call is at 6 a.m., count backwards. One hour of driving to set, 45 minutes shot list writing, thirty minutes for exercise, shower, dress, and breakfast. Alarm clock set at 4:45 a.m. Really.

My routine during production is I wake up, do the personal prep, boot the computer, and launch into my shot list. Here is what my shot list looks like.

DAY SEVEN DECOUPAGE

1.   **SCENE 13 - WAREHOUSE CHASE**

Up at Real Door

Action: REAL Mac comes through real door, wavers, lunges onto genie lift

Camera: On the ground, low angle **- B cam C/U, C Cam up behind Mac.**

2.   **M/S reveal Morgan up on real door - B cam C/U, C Cam up behind Morgan**

3.   **Stunt 'Mac'   real jump to post - 2 cams down, one up**

4.   **Stunt 'Morgan' swings off - 2 camsdown, one up**

5.   **Insert post bends**

6.   **Mac c/u lands, runs to stairs**

7.   **Mac on stairs M/S pan, & B cam XCU feet, face.**

How do I come up with this info?

The call sheet says first up is scene 11. Read scene 11 in your script. Make notes of the key story beats. If it's important that John is trying to hide his anger from Sue, that's a story beat. If he fingers the gun in his pocket, that's a beat. Then open your palmtop location file. Review your plot plan and shooting plan. Then start writing the shot list for that scene.

Who are you writing this info for? Who gets a copy? You, the DP, the AD, the key grip, the gaffer, the Sound Department, the script supervisor, possibly the PM. Call sheet aside your shot list is the real menu for the day. The battle plan.

Shot lists vary from director to director. My personal shot list first notes what scene we are cutting from so I'll know what the tone is. It notes what the cut in and the cut out is. I'll list the master shot, whether it's on track, sticks, Steadicam. I'll note if the shot goes from scene beginning to end. I'll note the story beats this shot must express.

I will note what B camera is doing. Often B cam notes will be less specific leaving B more open to creative improv.

Then I'll list any coverage I may desire, the close-ups and inserts. I note what part of the scene they will cover and what story beat must be expressed.

That's it. End of scene. Move on to what's next on the call sheet.

I number each set-up. When I get to the end of the call sheet if I find I have twenty-five setups and if I know from previous days' work (or if this is day one from soliciting the opinions of my keys on what they think the unit is capable of) that our unit can do only twenty set-ups without overtime, I know I either have to scale back or plan for overtime.

It's not uncommon for a director to put what's known as a "target of opportunity" on the shot list. On the off chance you finish early or can't film something you'd hoped to, the AD will be prepared to shoot your target.

For the crew version of my list I'll strip off all the cut from, cut to, story beat info and make up a simple shot list for the crew. I'll print a copy of each, cut it to fit in my pocket, and I'm out the door.

THE CIRCUS

The unit. That assembly of production trucks, trailers, catering vans, extras holding tents, generators, picture cars, crew cars, and equipment carts. This is what is known as the *Circus*. With good reason.

Before people went to the movies (or watched TV) they went to the circus. The circus brought the sights, sounds, smells of exotic foreign worlds into the lives of people who frequently never traveled more than a few miles from home their entire lives. Circus folk were exotic. They dressed outlandishly, behaved outrageously, and often had morals that could make a rabbit breeder blush. In other words, your average film set.

There will be a map on the back of the call sheet directing you to where the circus is today. As you draw near you'll see signs directing you to crew park and to the set.

You've Arrived

I first seek out the 3rd AD and give her a copy of the crew shot list for copying and distribution. She usually gives me pocket-sized sides (the scenes we're shooting this day). If catering is up I'll grab a coffee. I'll meet and greet whoever is around, then head up to set.

The First Look

It's never right. There is always something happening on your set when you first see it in the morning that, left unchecked, will cost you time and set-ups later in the day.

No matter how thoroughly you've briefed the crew on where the scene is or where the camera is going to be or where is safe to stow gear or how the furniture is arranged, invariably something is not where it should be. Get there early and it's no problem. A simple word to the FX guys that their smoke tube will be in shot and presto, it's gone and you've made a friend.

I walk through my sets visualizing each of the scenes looking through my viewfinder. This is my first time seeing it dressed. It looks different. Maybe my plan was flawed. Maybe the other side of the room is better in this light. I'll often ask the set dressers to flip the furniture in a set. Again if I'm there early, no problem.

If there are critical props on the set I will usually oversee their placement personally. The location of the pots and pans impacts on where the cutting board will be. Which impacts on where the murder weapon would likely be. If I don't make certain it's all where it should be we'll get to staging that part of the scene later in the day and the actor will say, *"But why would the knife be there?"* And there goes the time I need for one of my precious set-ups. Be there early and you're already ahead.

Welcoming the Cast

I always ask my AD department to alert me when various people arrive. I like to meet the DP and designer to talk about yesterday's dailies and to go over the work in front of us today. But most important, I need to know when the actors arrive at the circus.

I make it a point to seek out all the actors just to say hi each morning. But I actually visit with the lead actors when they arrive. Even if we're already shooting a scene they're not in. I'll make the effort to slip away during a lighting break. Why? Because it's a mark of respect. Plus I like actors enormously. Plus... *they are what the audience sees! They are telling my story!* Camera angles and great music mean little without a high-performance actor. If I have to, I'll settle for average in any department but acting. If the actor is uncomfortable, if they don't believe the words, if they're angry at their cos-tumer — it *shows!* Five minutes chatting with the leads as they're in makeup, asking how their kids are at home, talk-ing about a particularly good performance in last night's dailies, sharing a worry about today's line-up. This is not a huge sacrifice to make for the magic they bring us each day.

During the few moments I spend greeting the leads each morning I may also use the opportunity to bring them up to speed on my approach to what's up first. If it's a straightfor-ward scene in a location we both know I may ask the actor to give me their blessing to go ahead and block it without them. So they can remain in hair/makeup/wardrobe and thus get to camera faster. We've just saved thirty minutes. I'm one set-up ahead.

TIME TO ROLL

I'll often walk or ride up to set with the 1st AD. It gives us a chance to go over the first few scenes.

When we arrive on set all the pre-rigging should be done. Usually the DP will be there a few minutes before set call. Together the DP and I will visit the set alone. We'll quickly discuss our approach to the scene. This isn't just a start-of-day thing. I need this time alone with the DP prior to every scene.

The 1st AD will then say something like: *"Ding, ding. We're on the clock. Welcome to day (# whatever) of the fabulous production of (whatever). Our first deal, scene 11. In the study. John and Sue argue, Sue storms out. Charles, it's all yours."*

Show time.

This is it. The conductor faces the orchestra and raises the baton. From this moment forward it's for real. What I do next will have an unchangeable impact on what the audience sees.

I generally say something like, *"Morning, all. At this point in the story, Sue and John are quarreling. Sue has just heard John making a date with Ellen. Now in this scene we have John seated by the phone, having just hung up. Sue enters, paces, arguing. The set works best for light and background if we seat John somewhere around here and if we have Sue enter here and pace in this general area facing this way. The*

camera will be on this side moving in slowly. Any comments?
Okay, let's have a look. Blocking, and action."

The actors will try a run-through and I'll watch it looking
through my viewfinder. I move as I intend the camera to
move. The keys will watch us, each with a view to what
impact my plan will have on their department. When the
actors experience difficulty with some aspect of the set (which
happens), we'll pause and resolve the issue, then move on.

Once we're through it I'll mention my coverage plans, close-
ups here, inserts there. The DP will often have suggestions.
Perhaps the cast will volunteer something. We'll adjust then
run it again. The 1st AD will advise the camera assistant that
"This time it's for marks." We will stop and start the action,
giving the assistant a chance to put a mark down where we
wish an actor to pass through or stop. Each actor gets their
own color of mark.

Once we finish this the 1st AD will ask the DP if he's seen
enough to rig it. If so, the AD sends the cast away and says,
"The crew has the floor." The DP commences (or finishes if
it's been pre-rigged) lighting the shot.

Once the cast finishes with hair/makeup/wardrobe, while
the set is being lit, we'll get together and rehearse. We'll go
to the green room or our chairs or out in a field and run it
and run it. If there are problems we'll try to work them out
(more on that later). We'll run it until it's working. By
which time the AD will be calling us back to set.

Ready, Aim...

The actors take their places. The AD calls for final touches. Hair, makeup and wardrobe slip in and check the details. The director takes a seat at video village in front of the twin video monitors that display both A and B camera (if there's a B). The sound boom person gets into position. The camera operator and focus puller mount up onto the dolly. The dolly grip pushes the dolly to first position. The DP takes a final light reading and calls out the exposure to his 1st assistant, *"A thin 2.8."* The AD will call, *"Roll sound."* The mixer will confirm he's recording, the boom man will announce, *"Speed."* The AD will call, *"Roll camera."* The 1st assistant will start the camera and respond, *"Camera rolling, mark."* The 2nd or 3rd camera assistant will hold up the correctly marked slate, call out the scene and take numbers and say *"Mark."* They'll smack the clapper. The operator/s will set the opening frame then call out *"Frame."*

Now it's your turn. *"And... action."* The "and" is not an affectation. You're giving the cast and crew a few milliseconds to ramp up to speed rather than simply barking "action" and expecting everything to begin at once.

DIRECTING AS THE CAMERAS ROLL

The scene commences. The director watches the monitors. What exactly is the director watching for? There are so many people watching. The DP is watching for light, focus, and operation. The sound people are listening for clarity and overlaps. The script supervisor is watching to see that all the lines are delivered and who picks up what prop when. What's left for the director to watch for?

I have this thing I do just before a take. I close my eyes and mentally scroll at lightning speed through every shot that's happened in the script before this moment (the un-shot ones exist only in my imagination at this point). As I call for action I open my eyes and let the movie "resume."

Then I watch. What I'm looking for is, do I like this movie? Do I get what's going on? Does this shot fit into the movie? Am I learning something important I did not know before this moment?

> *The director is the only one on set who is actually watching the movie like the audience will.*

The director is the proxy audience. The director is the audience's lawyer. If I as the director don't feel something on screen serves my client's (the audience's) best interests — I object.

In the first take or two of the master, especially if it's a long scene, I will count the things that need improvement. That makes it easier to remember when I'm talking to the cast and crew between takes.

Who Gets To Say "Cut"?

The director. No one else. No exceptions.

When the take is over or something goes seriously wrong the director calls out *"cut"* and filming stops. Sometimes in a long take an actor will blow a line. Sometimes I'll call out *"keep rolling,"* and have the script supervisor prompt the actor. If the shot is what we call a "one-er," that is the entire scene shot in one uncut take with no close-ups or insert shots, when there's a mistake I cut and go again. But if I'm shooting coverage it's a judgment call. Some actors don't like being directed while the camera is rolling. I ask first.

Stop Start

Say someone gets killed midway through a master. Say that killing will be dealt with in separate stunt/FX shots. We'll often do something called stop and start. When the actor gets killed I'll call out, *"Everyone freeze. John, take your dead position. And... action."* And I resume the scene carrying through to the end. The advantage is that now I've got a master instead of owing an extra set-up. I then shoot all the actual dying details in coverage.

That Was Perfect – We're Going Again

Once you call cut you're faced with the decision of whether to take it again or move on. Your decision is based on whether you thought the actor's performances told the story believably and got the point across. It's also based on how well the take worked from the keys' various POVs. Of course you were keeping a third eye out for everyone else's stuff during the take.

When an operator or a sound person tells me the take was no good that means they want another. It's a good idea to ask, *"Which part was no good?"* Say this was a long master for which we'll be shooting coverage. If the flaw was at a point where I think we'll be into close-ups and if we're in a hurry, we move on. This can be a contentious area. We'll talk more about it later.

I'll often have notes for the camera operator. Delay this move. Pan over to catch her entrance faster, that sort of thing. I'll sometimes have blocking notes for the actors. More often I'll have insights into what they're trying to express and how better to express it. I give the notes and we go again.

How Demanding Can You Be?

Nothing is ever perfect. The cast always wants to do another. So does the camera operator. So does sound. But they generally have a less acute awareness of the pressures of time. On the other hand, if you habitually finish the day ahead of schedule the keys and the actors are going to be rightly concerned that you're not getting their best.

WORKING WITH THE DIRECTOR OF PHOTOGRAPHY

Many directors consider their on-set relationship with the DP to be the key creative relationship in the entire show. A friendly professional interaction is critical both to the smooth functioning of the set and to the look and feel of the finished film. The most complex emotions and the most subtle story beats are achieved through lighting, camera movement, framing, and exposure. But as with any intense relationship there is great potential for both harmony and conflict between the director and the DP.

I learned an important lesson on my first film. The DP and I fought like cats and dogs. He felt I didn't care about the look of the show. I felt he was working too slowly, essentially shooting his demo reel. We were both wrong. What we had neglected to do was sit down and agree upon how much time we had for each scene and stick to a schedule based on that. I was nervous. I think I probably pushed too hard, even when we were ahead.

Since then I've learned how to establish a *modus vivendi* with DPs. We essentially negotiate the ratio we're going to set between work time and shoot time. So I never have that situation you see on student sets so often where 95% of the time goes into building and lighting the shot then the director is rushed to do one or two quick takes and move on.

Every director/DP combo finds its own way to rock. Some DPs feel it's their job to design all the shots and some directors are happy to let them. Some directors design every shot and the DP lights. Whatever works. The important thing is communication and a clear understanding that *shotmaking is secondary to storytelling*. The look of the show is super important, but how often do you hear a movie patron or critic saying, *"Hey, the story sucked and the acting blew but man — what camera moves! Two thumbs up!"*

Finally, it's worth mentioning that there's an attitude some DPs have that doesn't fit real well into the collaborative enterprise that filmmaking is. It's best illustrated by the following tale.

A director dies and goes to heaven. She finds herself standing in line at St. Peter's Gate with another director. The line moves forward slowly. They notice a guy pushing his way to the front of the line. He's wearing a trendy crew vest, he has a few light meters and a viewfinder around his neck.. He shoves through the door in front of everyone. The one director pipes up: *"He gets to go first just because he's the DP?"* To which the other replies, *"No, that was God. He only thinks he's the DP."*

Funny story. Fortunately, it rarely happens. Most director/DP relationships are strong, creative partnerships that span years.

Charles works with DP Tobias Schliessler on **Quarantine**
Chris H. Benz Photo

Working With Stunts and FX

Stunts and FX people love their work. They're often like big kids in a sandbox. The enthusiasm most of them bring to your show can be infectious. But sometimes they're so anxious to give you their best that they're inclined to give too much. It's a rare stunt man or FX worker who offers up *less* than you want. Left to their own devices they generally go for bigger, louder, harder, faster. A popular FX crew shirt says, *"F!#$ the dialogue — Let's blow something up!"* Unless you let them know your intent in the action scenes, don't be surprised if they propose putting a car chase gun battle into *Driving Miss Daisy*. If the script says: *"Jim has a heart attack,"* don't let them give you three back flips with full-on chest exploding blood hits.

Working With Visual FX

This is far too complex a topic to even brush over here. And it changes from day to day as new technology comes on line. Many shows have visual FX. Some shows are so full of computer generated imagery (CGI) that the actors are shot against a screen and everything else is done in post. There will be one or more Vis FX consultants on-set when the FX oriented scenes are being filmed. Because the shooting for computerized processing is so precise, the director can find himself a bystander on his own set.

The way to approach this is to understand that the Vis FX crews work for the FX lab. It's in the FX lab's interest that you the director understand their process. They're usually happy to give you the tour, the demo, even a full-on workshop. They welcome you to come sit in the corner and watch. Learn the rules. Take control of the process.

The Tone

A week into prep the tone a show is going to have is pretty well fixed. If people are screaming in prep they'll probably scream on set too. If people are open, calm, and friendly in prep, that's likely how the shoot will go.

In the first few days of any shoot the cast and crew watch the director very carefully for cracks in the finish. The tone the director sets and maintains gradually washes over the entire production like the coat of transparent stain you brush onto that dining room table you once refinished. Some stains are harsh, ugly, opaque. Others are so thin and wishy-washy that all of the underlying defects glare through. A good stain covers everything with a rich, lustrous tone, bringing out the underlying beauty. It blends a bunch of boards into one beautiful whole.

That's Lunch

Lunch always comes too soon. There are union rules covering lunch issues. Say you're in the middle of a shot when lunch time comes and you haven't got a useable take yet. The AD asks the crew shop steward for something called "Grace." If granted this allows the director to try and get a useable take in a few more tries.

Once the unit breaks they take either a half hour or a full hour counted from the time the last person through the line is served. Lunch length is a crew-negotiated issue. From a director's point of view hour-long lunches are bad. All the energy drains out of the crew. They eat too much, start to snooze, then take an hour to get back up to speed.

At lunch with Denise Crosby
Kharen Hill Photo

The first people through the lunch line at the catering truck are usually the teamsters. They always park their clubhouse on wheels strategically between craft service and catering.

The next people to appear in the lunch line are the actors. Most of the cast is mind numbingly idle most of the time. When it's lunch, they're there like... like actors at a catering truck.

Next, the set crew that needs to be back on set first are ushered in by the ADs. The director will be in there somewhere. Then the rest of the cast and crew. Extras are last.

Resist the urge to crash the line. The people in the food line will often offer you the chance to move ahead of them. Don't do it. As polite and friendly as their gesture may be there's a risk you'll be seen as thinking you're more important than they are. If you really need to do stuff at lunch ask your AD to have a plate made up and sent to your trailer ahead of time.

At lunch I always check messages, call home and do any producer calls I need to do. My family likes to hear from me. And producers often like to hear how stuff is going from the horse's mouth.

We're Back

The director and AD will have spoken during the lunch break. We will have discussed how far ahead or behind we might be for the day. If we feel we're behind, it's often good to get the first shot of the afternoon done quickly. It lets the food know we mean business about digestion. And it sets a pace for the afternoon.

That first morning went by in a bit of a blur. We didn't have much time to talk about shooting style. Let's do that now.

THE DIRECTOR'S MEDIUM
Obviously, every director has a different artistic style. And each script calls for a different stylistic approach. Stylistic issues are generally thought to be a function of the artistic

needs of the story, and especially the talent of the director. That's why Ridley Scott gets paid more than the director who did *Gladys the Talking Mule*, right?

The reality that working directors know to be so true it goes without saying is that business pressures frequently play a greater role in the artistic realization of a project than... well, art.

Those who have never been in the trenches as a hired director rarely have much awareness of this. What film or TV critic ever blames budget or schedule or network issues for a show's shortcomings? How often does a reviewer invest the two minutes it would take on *Imdb.com* to learn that all of this producer's other shows have been critical failures and that this current director actually managed to rise above.

Here's an example. I recently wrote a draft for another director for a movie based on true crime events. The incredible details of the story had been well covered in the media. The script pitched itself. All the rights were secured. It was green lit. The fate of the project came down to one network creative authority who insisted that the true crime genre wasn't testing well. That unless we turned away from the remarkable events and went for what he felt was more of a "character piece" the greenlight would go red. So who was the real *auteur* on this picture?

Shooting Style

A director who has fifteen days to shoot a 90-minute TV movie must adjust the *pace* of work to fit that schedule. But the director must also consciously adopt a shooting *style* to fit that schedule. The most common shooting style for a project like this would be a simple *master/coverage* style. A master shot with close-ups.

A director who has eighty days to shoot a studio film has the luxury to choose a different style, a common one being what is sometimes referred to as the *sub-master style*. This is where an overall master may not be shot at all. Instead a series of sub-masters are shot for each emotionally different section of the scene. Then appropriate coverage (two-shots, close-ups, inserts, etc.) is shot for each sub-mastered section. Obviously this technique is much more time consuming. It's also much more capable of finding the subtle emotional beats as the characters act and react throughout the scene.

Shooting style also changes with different cast and crew members. A difficult actor or one with a poor memory for lines or marks is not going to give their best in a long, complex master. Likewise, a camera department with a less than gifted operator or focus puller is not going to give their best with those aesthetically beautiful long lenses one might otherwise use.

What Cast and Crew Want

Many actors and directors prefer long, complex master shots that make use of only a limited amount of coverage. A long master gives them a chance to create a mood, control the pace, tell the story. By contrast, cutting a scene up into short takes makes it more difficult to maintain emotional continuity and progression. Crews respect intelligent master shots. Because they require skill and training to execute.

Ideally one would shoot a cinematic master, then shoot just enough coverage to allow the scene to be adjusted for pace, meaning, and emphasis later on in post. Why doesn't everybody shoot this way?

Obviously, no director intentionally sets out to shoot a boring master. But trying to do otherwise is really challenging. What if you invest a morning in blocking, lighting and rehearsing a complex master only to find that an actor keeps blowing a line or missing a mark? What if your operator just can't make the camera move. Or your focus puller keeps getting it soft? What if you get up to take 15, and they still can't get it right but insist on doing it over and over until they do? Over and over and over....

Some directors respond to this fear by risking little with their master. They'll put most of their effort into cutting it up into bite-sized pieces. They concentrate on getting enough coverage to make it happen in editing. One of my favorite executive producers, Don S. Williams, refers to this shooting style as the "monkey at the typewriter" approach.

A more cinematic method is to commit to as intelligent a master shot as seems realistically achievable within the constraints of the project, and then cover as needed.

MASTER/COVERAGE

When you're channel surfing on your TV, master/coverage is recognizable at a glance. Every scene starts close on a phone or something, then pulls back into a static wide shot. Cut to medium close-up. Ping pong back and forth on medium close-ups for a while. Then into close-ups. Back out to the static master once to remind us of the geography. Then cut to close on the actor's pensive stare for scene end.

The argument is made that it's the safest way of filming actors saying and doing stuff such that a general audience will get the general drift. But much more than that: it is an *industrial system*. In the same way that an automobile assembly line is. When producers demand coverage they are demanding *components*. Engines, fuel pumps, tail lights. In episodic TV the components one director shoots are frequently installed in other director's shows. Parts compatibility.

In this system the real act of "creation" happens mainly in the editing room when the various components are assembled. The components can be assembled in many different ways. Some of them far from anything the director ever imagined.

Creative Coverage

There are tricks to make coverage more interesting. One is to block the scene with a lot of business. Instead of two people sitting talking have one or both of them busy clearing off the dishes from the table or reading the paper, knitting, watching TV, pacing. Anything appropriate to the mood. If the subject is moving, the close-ups are automatically more dynamic. And if the actors have business you can always cut away to an insert of the knitting or whatever, which will often redefine what's really going on in the scene.

A second camera can work wonders with coverage. If you have two cameras and if you must shoot master/coverage it's often not possible to shoot a good close-up angle on an actor with the B cam while the A cam is shooting the master. The B can rarely get a perfect angle. The light is usually wrong. Frequently the A cam drifts into B's frame on the dolly. So what does the B cam do while A shoots the master?

It goes fishing.

The director can ask the B cam operator to try interesting moves. The kinds of creative shots you'll never have time to set up and execute properly with the A cam. In this way you just may get some very spontaneous and creative shots. You may also get a lot of re-frames, out of focus shots, and unusable material. But the trade-off is often well worth it.

One major caution with this strategy. Be straight with your sound people. If your hope is to get the scene in an interesting master with some exciting B camera grabs, quietly let the sound mixer know that. Otherwise they'll assume you are shooting close-ups and may not be as fussy over sound quality on the master. More than once I've felt joy telling the unit we've just shot a terrific one-shot scene and then looked up to see a freaked out sound mixer storming over sputtering, *"But... you said..."*

Pulling the Plug

Airplane pilots have a decision point picked out on the runway before they commence take-off. They know that if they're not airborne by that point they have just enough runway left for a panic stop. Continuing to attempt take-off beyond the decision point *might* result in a successful take-off. It could also result in a fiery death. Guess which one they usually choose.

A director facing the complex master situation needs a decision point as well. To decide how much time to invest in blocking, lighting, and shooting a complex master, the director needs to discuss with the AD what the maximum time shooting this scene can take. Let's say you've got to be out of it by 4 p.m.

Calculate how much time you'd need to abandon the plan and shoot enough coverage to get the scene. Say that's three hours. So 1 p.m. is your decision point.

As you near 1 p.m. questions need to be asked and answered. How close are they to getting it? Say it's take 6 and you've already got a couple of otherwise useable takes with some minor problems. If both cast and crew are performing well you're in pretty good shape. Quietly tell your AD that if we don't get it in two or three more takes we'll move on.

But if you're on take 20 and the actor keeps missing lines or the operator keeps blowing a move, pull the plug.

The Let Down

It's hard to pull the plug on a sequence like this. The cast and crew have a tendency to interpret your pragmatic choice as a vote of non-confidence in them. They feel they've failed the director. Occasionally operators will plead or actors will demand another one. For the young director faced with an experienced cast or crew this situation can be intimidating.

But the director is the pilot. Pilots don't poll their passengers to see who needs to get there so badly they're prepared to take unacceptable risks. Neither does a director.

WORKING WITH SOUND

Which brings us to another common director/crew conflict: sound. Sound mixers sit at a little cart off to one side. Sometimes in another room entirely. They watch the camera feed through a tiny black-and-white monitor. But their real window on the world is their headphones. They communicate with their boom operator via a small talkback mike. Sound mixers often act like they're not part of the unit. There's a good reason. They have to be "blind" and apart.

Humans are visually oriented. We pay far more attention to the sensory input we receive through our eyes than that which we receive through our ears. Most people on and off a film set know very little about sound. Few people listen very closely to sound in real life. But put them in front of a movie and watch how quickly they get restless if the sound is muggy. Or if the dialogue is hard to understand, distorted, out of sync.

On set it's rare that anyone will complain if the DP says we need thirty minutes to put up more lights. But let the sound mixer ask for five minutes to put up a blanket or adjust a radio mike and suddenly we're under the gun. We gotta roll. Come *on*.

There's always pressure to relegate sound issues to the back burner. This can be a terrible mistake. There is no substitute for good location sound. Crew people often say, *"You can't ADR the picture. Dub it later."* And on a giant budget show this is almost true. But for the majority of shows, if you get poor dialogue recorded on set the show will suffer badly. The reason is simple. Looping, ADR (automated dialogue replacement) is difficult and expensive to do well. People may tell you different. They're mostly wrong. Here's why.

Looping

Looping (so called because the actual film used to be spliced into a loop so it could run through the projector over and over again) goes like this: It's 9 a.m. An actress comes into the studio with a cup of coffee. She's greeted by the engineer and the sound editor. Frequently the director is off directing his next show. The engineer hands the actress a list of lines that need replacing. The actress enters the booth and stands up to the mike. She's asked for a few words to get a sound level. Then the engineer hits play. The actress watches herself on the screen. She listens to the original line that needs replacing. She watches it once or twice, then say she's ready. The engineer hits record. The actress watches the screen and attempts to say the line with the exact same pacing and spacing as she did when it was filmed. She'll take it a number of times. Occasionally the editor might say something like, "*Try one with a bit more feeling.*" Once they get one that seems to fit *visually* it's on to the next loop. What's wrong with this picture?

Looping Turns Everything Into a Foreign Film

Cinefiles often refuse to watch foreign films that have been dubbed into English. The reasons are obvious. The original performance is lost forever, replaced by someone with a cup of coffee standing in a booth at 9 a.m. Exterior scenes are recorded *inside* and they sound that way. Scenes shot in a giant hall are recorded in a tiny booth and they sound that way. A scene that was shot with a number of actors guided by a director, feeling the set, feeling each other, feeling the pure chemistry of a group performance, screaming, whispering, laughing — all this is gone forever.

On high-budget shows the studio can demand that the performances be recreated. The mixing facility will have the money to pull in all kinds of high-tech resources. So much talent and money is thrown at the problem that they can get really close to what was lost. And the actors get the time and direction to recreate their performance, sometimes even to improve it. But many shows are running low on budget by the time they get to post sound. The effort is almost never made. The show suffers.

We often shoot in locations that for one reason or another have not been chosen with good clean sound in mind. We often haven't got time to retake indefinitely until there's clean sound. But anyone who's spent much time on set knows that there's a tendency to denigrate the importance of location sound. People who have never spent five minutes in a looping session will say, *"It's good enough for guide track. Gotta move on."* A good director doesn't buy into this.

What a good director does is establish a dialogue with the sound mixer. Make it a habit to include the sound guys in your blocking discussions. Suggest mike placement if it's a difficult angle and the mixer is receptive. Tell the mixer when you shoot a wide master and tight B cam coverage on the same take — a mixer's nightmare because he can't get the boom in close. Choose to either radio mike the B cam subject or do another one on B cam alone. And finally in a case where you don't have time to do it right for sound, explain why and hope for their best under difficult circumstances.

THE SCRIPT SUPERVISOR

The script supervisor or continuity person is responsible for continuity. Which hand held the cigarette? What should the clock say? That sort of thing. Keeping track of all these details in a moving scene with a half dozen actors can be very demanding for her (the overwhelming majority of script supervisors are women, no idea why). But that's not all the script supervisor is doing.

She is also following each line of dialogue in the script. If an actor misses or changes a line the script supervisor notifies the director. Frequently the director will empower the script supervisor to prompt the actors during a take when they forget their lines.

On top of this, she is responsible for making extensive notes in the script and in the logs she turns in to the editor. Those notes include how many takes of each shot were done, what parts of the scene were covered by what shots, what lens and aperture were used, what camera roll, sound roll, and any relevant production notes. In editing, all of the information the editor has about everything on the shoot comes through the script supervisor. Tough job.

Be friends with your script supervisor.

Because she makes the notes she is the messenger. So the script supervisor is sometimes blamed for the message by producers and network executives. *"Why the hell didn't you shoot a close-up? How the hell come you changed that line?"* A script supervisor can react to these unreasonable pressures by passing them on to the director. In TV it's not uncommon for the script supervisor to adopt the role of script cop. She can pop up and ask for another take whenever something happens she knows she'll get hell for. This can seriously affect a director's spontaneity.

A common battle ground is the *overlap* issue. When two or more people are talking it's natural for them to interrupt each other. To overlap their words on top of each other's. Script supervisors (and sound mixers) are trained to hate overlaps. Because it makes sound editing more difficult. If you're shooting a close-up of Mary and we hear Andy's dialogue on top of hers, how does the editor cut for performance and pacing? But when the director intends to run the shot uncut, overlaps are often okay. It's extremely irritating to have the script supervisor constantly requesting additional takes because of overlaps. I ask the actors to "watch the overlaps" when we're shooting coverage. But when we're doing one-shot sequences I advise the script supervisor to check with me before speaking up. And simply make the note on her report that the director was advised of this particular continuity crime and chose to accept it. This at least solves the problem for the short term.

A far better solution is to get the script supervisor on your team. Think about it. She sits right beside the director at the monitor all day. She has a better vantage point from which to watch and understand the director's approach than anyone else on set. If the director were to choose one best friend on set, who better?

I always have a meeting with the script supervisor in prep, even on an episodic TV show. I let her know I value and respect her opinion. I tell her I see our working relationship as a collaboration. I invite her to have fun with me on the show. More often than not this results in me having someone to bounce stuff off on set. Someone without a vested interest I can ask for advice on a particular take. And if I get into trouble I have a second brain helping me dig out. In short, the script supervisor is at my side *on* my side.

COOL TOOLS — DIRECTOR PROTOCOL
In the 1980 film *The Stunt Man,* a movie about a movie being filmed, the director played by Peter O'Toole is shown swooping around the film set, God-like on an enormous crane —

joyriding. Who hasn't seen images of Francis Coppola wearing the combat helmet riding a gunship chopper in *Apocalypse Now*? Or James Cameron riding in the submarine down to the *Titanic*. Most photos of directors have them standing with gear. Eye to the Panaflex, riding the dolly.

You as the director have the authority to look through the camera and reframe, recompose any time you want. You have the authority to ride the dolly, the crane, the chopper, even the stunt car. But there's a fairly rigid protocol.

The Rules for the Tools

> 1. Don't hurt anyone.
>
> 2. Don't waste time.
>
> 3. Don't make a fool of yourself.

That's it. All the observations that follow are illustrations of how to follow these rules. Seasoned directors may want to skim most of this.

Looking Through the Camera

Should you look through the camera? After all, video village is comfortable. You can see what the operator has framed in your monitor. Why interfere with the camera crew? The obvious answer is that sometimes it's faster and easier to *show* the operator than to tell him.

The protocol is as follows: As a shot is being set up, wait for the grips and the camera assistants to set the camera up where it's going to be. On the tripod, on the dolly, wherever.

Stand near the camera to let them know you want a look. But give them time and space to set up and level it. This is where the operator will ask you what lens you'd like to see. Once the operator begins looking through the camera but before he gets the assistant to start getting focus marks, ask him, *"Can I have a quick look, please?"*

The operator will give you the camera with the viewfinder open, focused to your particular eye with the lens aperture open wide and the tripod locks loose enough to permit your adjustment of the frame. If he docsn't, let him know that this is what you expect.

Have a look. Get oriented. Reframe to taste. Lock the tripod. Give it back to the operator and say, *"Something like that."* The operator may tweak what you've done but now he knows what you're after.

The caution here is that whenever the director takes over the camera, *everybody watches*. If you don't improve on what the operator had initially they're likely to think you're a bit of a poser.

Riding the Dolly

Same story with the dolly but even more so. Because everyone can see that the dolly is fun to ride. If you ask to have a ride on the dolly then offer up little by way of shot improvement, what was the point to this time you just wasted? A legitimate occasion for the director to ride on the dolly is when you have several story beats that need connecting and the planned dolly shot simply isn't doing the job.

Charles setting up a shot
Kharen Hill Photo

The protocol is this: As soon as the camera is ready on the dolly advise the camera/grip crew, *"I'd like to take a ride please."* Ask your AD for stand-ins so you can see people in your shot. The operator will get off and you will get on. You'll ask the dolly grip to take you to "first position." Once there, frame up what you see as the shot opening, advising the stand in/s where to be. Then say, *"That's 1st position."* The camera assistant will put marks down for the actor, the dolly grip will put down his mark, the operator will be watching the monitor, learning your intent. Then tell the dolly grip to start the move. Tell the stand-in, *"Action."* Work your way through to the 2nd position. Ask for everyone to stop. Advise this is 2nd position. And so on as you compose your shot down the line.

There's no point being overly fussy with precise framing or smooth operation. That's the operator's job. When you get to the end, thank the grip. Give it back to the operator asking, *"Is that clear?"* He may have observations or suggestions. For example he may ask if he can tuck an invisible zoom into the move to keep what you need in the shot. That sort of thing.

Riding The Crane

Exact same deal with the crane except even more so. Because while the crane is a lot of fun to ride it's also an extremely complex tool. An inexperienced director can waste a lot of time fumbling around on one. Plus there are safety issues. If you're going to ride it you'd better come up with some great ideas while you're up there. Know how many production reports go back to the PM/producer with a note like *"1/2 hr idle while dir played on crane...."*

The protocol: Advise the AD and operator you'd like a ride. The operator will advise the crane grip. Many cranes have *counterweights* that need adjustment to your weight before you can get airborne. It's critical that you listen carefully and follow the grip's exact instructions when getting on or off. If you upset the delicate balance of the rig, *several thousand pounds of steel come crashing down onto the crew*. This also could look bad on the production report.

When the grip advises you to get on, do so. He'll often put a safety belt on you. Then put your eye to the camera and request he take you (and the stand ins) to 1st position. If you're inexperienced or have issues with heights don't take your eye away from the viewfinder. It can be alarming. Go through the exact same procedure you'd use on the dolly. Compose the shot. When it's time to get off, listen to and follow the grip's instructions to the letter.

Planes, Trains and Automobiles

They're all camera-carrying vehicles. But the bigger they are the more dangerous, expensive, and time consuming. So it's even more important that you have communicated your vision during prep via conversation, storyboards, and an exact shot list on the day.

All of the above notwithstanding, you have the right and responsibility to utilize the tools in the toolbox to the best of your ability. Frequently the best way to do this is to take the camera and have a look around. Riding the crane, a good director always spins around looking for other cool stuff. Any time the director puts their eye to the eyepiece there's always the potential for coming up with something fresh and new. The very fact that the director *isn't* a professional operator or pilot or driver is often what gives them a way of conceptualizing a shot that an expert would never think of.

Just be aware that a tremendous amount of time can be consumed getting on and off the damn devices. If your rationale is simply to "have a look see," save the time. Leave it to the pros.

Operator Dean Friss and Charles shooting green screen on ABC-TV
Angel Flight Down
Tina Schliessler Photo

When the Director Isn't the Boss

It's critical to note that while the director has a great deal of authority on set, when it comes to moving vehicles (and stunts and FX) there are other crew people whose authority supersedes the director's.

Say you're shooting from the specialized crew-carrying camera car. When the operator or grip advises the director to buckle into a safety harness this is not debatable. It's an *order* the director must follow. Otherwise the operator can and will refuse to move. Likewise, the director can't hop on or off to chat with an actor whenever the spirit moves him. There are various signals used for stopping, starting, and so on. Again, the grip in concert with the AD will dictate this.

In the case of aviation, particularly with helicopters, the director is under the authority of the pilot, at all times. The pilot will tell you how and when to approach the craft, how and when to exit, and how to conduct yourself while on board. Even the director's artistic directions are subject to the overriding authority of the pilot. If a director requests something the pilot feels exceeds acceptable safety margins, the pilot can and will refuse the request.

Playing With the Toys

Movies frequently have cool toys in them. Planes, fast cars, bikes, whatever. So obviously that stuff is going to be found on a lot of movie sets. And frequently the transportation department will encourage the director to have some fun. Should you?

This can be iffy. I went for a ride in an unbelievably powerful Shelby Cobra on a show just for fun. And it was a lot of fun. The lead actor then asked if he could. He ended up in the ditch. Whoops.

I've since learned that the best policy is to keep a low profile. If I can quietly duck out of the lunch line and take the latest Porsche for a spin without making a big thing out of it, who's hurt?

Speaking of which, these toys are usually dangerous. That's what makes them fun. Say the director takes the Porsche out, hits a tree, breaks some bones. The entire production grinds to a very expensive halt. Frequently director insurance policies specify that dangerous behavior is not covered. Imagine how quickly the word will get around that you were replaced for goofing off on set. A director who spends a lot of time playing on set creates the impression that they don't take the work very seriously. Try to imagine Woody Allen zipping around set on a Harley.

It's best if you concentrate on doing the job. Play on your own time. But we're human. If it's a once in a lifetime opportunity — to visit the *Titanic* in a submarine, say — take a camera. Get some useable footage. Enjoy the ride.

SECOND UNIT

If the director's authority is limited when shooting from dangerous craft why bother even going? Why not let 2nd unit worry about it? In fact many directors do just that. But there are pitfalls here as well.

The 2nd unit is a reduced crew with a separate director, DP, AD, the various crafts, and especially the stunt team. The 2nd unit does not work with actors. Their job is to do the time consuming, dangerous, often remote work that it makes little sense to have the main unit shoot. On large action films the 2nd unit's schedule can be as long as that of the main unit.

2nd unit can be a contentious issue. Sometimes the 2nd unit director is hired by the PM without consulting the director. He's often a stunt man, a camera operator, an AD. Someone whose primary skills do not lie in the area of storytelling. And even though the material he shoots may not conform to the director's overall vision of the show, it is sometimes edited in and released under the director's credit.

I was watching 2nd unit dailies on a picture I was doing. I had provided the 2nd unit director precise instructions for what was needed. Specifically insert shots in an extremely realistic and panic-stricken gun fight. In dailies I was horrified to see a series of takes of a random gunman running toward camera, two guns out and blazing, Tarantino style. Multiple blood hits erupting from his chest. I asked the 2nd unit director what exactly he was thinking. He told me he thought it looked cool....

Sometimes producers who wouldn't dream of letting a non-factory trained mechanic work on their BMW will routinely let someone with no storytelling skills direct important sequences in their films and TV shows.

The Solution

There isn't one. So deal with it. Be polite and friendly to whomever it's expedient for them to give you. Try to impress upon the 2nd unit director what the story beats are. Make concise shot lists. Watch his dailies and correct them the second he starts improvising. Of course the real solution is for producers to involve the director in the hiring of one of the many highly trained 2nd unit directors that are always short of work. And of course that's what good producers try to do.

SCRIPT CHANGES ON SET
Partway through the afternoon everything's going great. And then suddenly we hit a wall.

We're in the middle of blocking a complex scene with a number of actors. There's a bunch of physical business, say cooking and eating. We've got entrances and exits. We're setting up a wonderful master that will eliminate the need for all the POV coverage a dinner scene normally requires. Suddenly an actor stops and says those fateful words: *"I'm sorry. My character wouldn't do this."* And it all comes to a screeching halt.

What do you do?

1. First the director usually says something like, *"It's working fine for me."* No sale.

2. Then the director will offer a cosmetic change: *"I see your point. Hmmm. How about if you came in through that door instead?"* No sale.

3. This is getting serious. Now the director starts damage control. *"Okay, let's just finish blocking and we'll work on it somewhere else while the crew finishes lighting."* To which the actor replies, *"What's the point of lighting me in places where I don't even know why I'm going?"* Damn.

Welcome to one of the director's worst nightmares. Set Screenwriting 101 in full view of the cast and crew. The first thing to do is get the AD involved. They should call a short break and clear the set while we get it worked out. An audience for this kind of thing only increases the tension and hardens everyone's position.

And sometimes if we take the problem seriously enough to clear the set the problem turns out to be less severe than imagined. A bit of discussion, a few subtle line changes, a shift in emphasis here and there, and the actor will realize that this is about as good as it's going to get. Problem solved.

This is a strong argument for working at being tight with the cast. I've had situations where I knew the actor was right. I disagreed with the script element in question myself. I knew how to cut around it in post. And I just didn't have the time to deal with it. I just said, *"Look, you've got to trust me on this one. I know this is wrong. But make yourself do the best you can with it and I promise you I'll make it right in post."* We shot the scene and went on.

But it doesn't always go that way. Sometimes people dig in their heels.

Occasionally it's because the actor has been angered by a specific thing. Maybe a costume is bothering them. Maybe their trailer is awful. Stuff I could have learned if I'd had a coffee with them when they came in this morning. Less often the actor is feeling insecure and argumentative just because they're psycho or bored, a pure mind game, the "script problem" is a figment of their imagination.

Hollywood lore abounds with horror stories of psychotic episodes with actors who wouldn't come out of their trailer. Or refuse to say certain lines. Or otherwise terrorize productions, all out of sheer insanity. I was on a set recently where a legendary Hollywood actress hated the producer and director so much she told the grip to erect a big black flag between her and the video monitors so she wouldn't have to see their faces. I spoke with her. She was charming, sensitive, and *very* angry. Know what she was ruining the show over? The producer had put her up way out of town and wouldn't give her a driver on the weekend. A few hundred dollars.

I've been lucky. I've worked with my share of allegedly "difficult" actors. But like Will Rogers I've never met an actor I didn't like. My experience is that actors *hate* to screenwrite on set. They *want* to do the scene and move on. But when something is wrong *they know they're the ones who ultimately will have to wear it*. How many times have you heard someone say things like, "*I hated Uma Thurman in* Kill Bill. *She was so stupid. Why didn't she just bring a gun?*"

People Rarely Argue Over a Scene That's Working

The most common reason actors hold up production over a script issue is, they're right. The scene makes no sense. The director complained about it in prep. But the writer/producers dug in their heels. The director said, "*How am I going to ask an actor to say and do these things? What's his motivation?*" The writer/producer's easy answer was "*Um, money?*" Well, here we are. You figure the actor is motivated by money? Really? Should we offer him a few bucks to shut up and get back to work? It doesn't work that way. But to say the actor is right rarely means he knows how to fix it. He just knows it's broken. So how do we fix it and move on?

The director will have a call put in to the producer to let him know there's trouble in paradise. The producer will often go through the condemned man's seven stages of denial before he begins a process of negotiation. How little change will the offending cast member settle for? The director in this case takes on the thankless role of a mediator running back and forth between the Palestinians and the Israelis. Finally a solution will be negotiated and accepted. Result: a considerable delay, an undermined director, an actor who's discovered a great new tool for next time, and a truncated scene. Lose lose.

There's Got To Be a Better Way

If the director has earned the producer's confidence the way forward is much clearer. You take the cast aside and go through the scene beat by beat. Lay it out. Let's say you're remaking *Gone With the Wind*. You're shooting the last scene. Scarlett is finally prepared to tell Rhett the truth but the actress is feeling a little weird about doing it with the defeated Confederate army looking on in the background. And the actor playing Rhett feels stupid just standing there. He wants some dialogue.

It's often not that hard to pinpoint what's ruining a scene. It's actions or words or a combination of both. "I *wouldn't do or say that*." Actions are the less difficult of the two — do something else. But when it comes to the words, searching for pithy dialogue often slows the whole process to a crawl. Actor Michael Beihn taught me an effective way to break this log jam. He calls it the "stick man" approach. Instead of trying to write good dialogue as you discuss scene fixing, just say "stick man."

So if the actors playing Scarlett and Rhett realize by working the scene with you that the extras can be framed out and Rhett has to say something, 9 times out of ten your actor will say something like, *"Okay and then after Scarlett tells me she really loves me and all that stuff I look at her and say 'stick man version' — Hey Babe, who gives a shit?"* Great. Now we very quickly find an end line that's a bit more in character, *"Honestly my love, I don't give a crap."* Something like that.

There's another type of problem. Many actors have a knack for zeroing in on that specific thing in the script that's forcing their character to do things their character wouldn't do. But what happens when that thing is something that *really needs to happen* for the story to go forward?

Say the script has Scarlett's character doing something inconsistent but the story won't work without it. Solution: *Try giving it to someone else in the scene*. Almost certainly there is another actor in the scene for whom this particular bit of behavior or dialogue would be much more in character. Let *them* do it. Result: a short delay, a cast that knows their director is a story teller, an improved scene. Win win.

Earning the producer's trust and respect is critical. If the director has been cavalier toward script change in prep or if you came in with poorly thought out ideas, the writer/producer knows the director has little respect for their script. It's a prep note but this is where the rubber meets the road.

It's never too late to earn the producer's trust. Get the producer on the phone and explain the problem. Suggest a conservative solution. But respectfully let the producer do their job. Sooner or later trust will grow.

Shooting Cuttable Stuff

Sometimes the director can try to get the actor to say and do what's in the script PLUS some other stuff the actor or director feels will make it work. But only if the other stuff is cuttable and takes very little time to shoot.

I once had an antagonist who was convinced his motivation in a scene should be that in the backstory the leading lady had rejected his advances. I considered it a confusing idea. But we were tight for time. So I let him do it and he turned in a remarkable performance. When the producer asked me what was going on I said, a) the extra material is fully cuttable and b) that motivation helped his performance come to life. The producer said, *"Good answer."*

Shoot It Both Ways

I did a sci-fi show where the lead character played by Ice T was locked up in a virtual prison. His solitary confinement cell existed only in his mind. My intention was to shoot the inside of the cell from the prisoner's POV: cell walls, bars, rats, etc. But from the outside, from the other prisoner's POV, he would just be sitting on a pedestal. No walls, no bars, nothing. The point would be made in juxtaposing the two points of view. It was a cool idea.

The trouble started when the art department asked me what color to paint the *outside of* the cell. I said don't bother. We'll never see it. The designer called the producer who called me. His position, *"Well, how are the other prisoners going to know he's in solitary?"* Huh? I discussed it with him. I debated it, argued it. Finally, I strained our relationship by asking if we could shoot it both ways. We did. Problem solved.

Sometimes that's the best you can do. But shooting like this wastes time and gives everyone clear proof that there's creative disunity among those steering the ship.

It's Just So Wrong

Sometimes a director is put into a position where you have to shoot something you know is totally wrong. Something you know is going to harm the project. There's a way to deal with this too.

Hit your mental Fast Forward button. Visualize yourself in the editing room a few days/weeks/months from now. Visualize yourself and the editor tearing out your hair and trying to cut around this heinous mistake. Visualize the editor saying, *"If only you had shot a _____ ."* Now fill in that blank. What's in that blank? Here's where your friendship with the script supervisor could pay off. Ask her to suggest something. Make a game out of it. Because there is always *something* you can shoot that will quietly save the scene.

Over My Dead Body

Sometimes in cases like this a director will feel so strongly he is right that he will do the unthinkable. He will simply shoot it the way he wants and to hell with the consequences.

In James Clavell's heroic novel *Shogun* the Blackthorne character claims that ignoring the will of your commander isn't treason *as long as you win*. And of course that's the lure of treason on a film set. As the director you know that if you do what you've been told the show could be ruined. Whereas if you take the law into your own hands the show will be saved. Or so the thinking goes.

This is a no-brainer. When you're in a situation where you're considering on-set treason ask yourself: If I do this will the show win an Oscar, an Emmy, or a Palm d'Or? *Will*

*independent and very loud voices acknowledge the rightness
of my choice such that my future employment is secure?*

Think about it. If this is an episode in the series *Beach Girls*
the only meaningful review you're ever going to get is the next
call from this producer or network. Think they're going to
call the person who defied them?

DIRECTING STARS

Directing stars is like directing actors only more so. On a
star-driven project the star knows that they are the reason
you're all here. And the reason *they* are here is to be great
in a successful piece of work and thereby continue being a
star. As long as they believe that their director is accom-
plishing that all will likely be well. But the minute they feel
that their director is compromising that goal there will likely
be conflict.

It's that simple. It's that complex.

The Shooting Stars

On the way up most directors meet stars who are on the way
down. Sometimes spectacularly so. How does a director handle that? I suggest with gentleness and respect. If you are
honest with yourself you have to admit that regardless of this
person's ability to do you any particular good they have scaled
a peak you haven't. And possibly never will. If your love for
the entertainment business is genuine, that alone should
command the respect due them.

When I meet a star, regardless of the current rating accord-
ed them by the anonymous list makers and gossips on the

E-shows, I always try to find an honest way to say something like, *"It's a real honor to meet you. I'm excited to be working with you. I can't thank you enough for the pleasure I've had watching your work."*

The Comeback Kid

There was a time not that long ago when John Travolta could be hired for scale. I don't mean you should be nice to people because of the good they may someday do you. Being straight with people generally makes them straight with you. I say it to illustrate a) how durable star quality is and b) how fallible the list makers can be.

I did a network show in the Canadian Rockies. At the wrap party the script supervisor I had particularly enjoyed working with introduced her boyfriend to me — Eric something. The party was crazy. Somebody got a karaoke thing going on. I was standing with Eric when it started. A grip was already up doing a black soul James Brown thing. Really embarrassingly. I groaned and said, *"Play that funky music white boy."* Eric said come on. Let's try. It'll be fun. I didn't think so. He got up and dedicated a song he sang to me, "Play That Funky Music White Boy." It was great, I was sold. We all got up and sang the night away. God it was fun. Eric sang numerous times. I thought I could detect in him the glimmerings of talent. I told his girl so. She agreed and told me he used to be in some Canadian TV series that had been cancelled. I felt kind of sorry for him. A few years later I saw my first episode of *Will and Grace....*

Stars, rising or falling, are people. Some you'll hit it off with. Others not. You'll do fine as long as you try to be straight, fight for your vision, listen, and learn.

Non-Actors

Sometimes you'll find yourself working with non-actors for one reason or another. Sometimes the freshness they bring can really enhance the show. One thing to remember: These people often don't know our jargon or understand our methods. Be direct.

On my first feature we found a local hot-rodder in the small town we were working who had a cinematic car and an interesting look. I wrote him into the background of the story. Everything he did played very well. Finally I decided to ask him to become a speaking character. The problem was we had no budget to pay anyone so I felt a little hesitant about asking. I took him aside and said something like, *"Um, Mike, ah... I wonder if maybe you might want to do a couple of lines with Pete and Tina."* His instant answer: *"Heck no. I stay away from the powder."* Be direct.

Death in the Afternoon

What everyone on the unit looks forward to as the afternoon wears on is that we'll work at a steady pace all day and finish five minutes before wrap. An early wrap, even if it's only five minutes early can be a huge psychological boost. It doesn't always work out that way.

Real trouble rarely comes in the morning. Even if it does, you generally aren't faced with the consequences until the afternoon. The clock begins to loom large. It's becoming clear that the time you spent rewriting that scene this morning is actually gone. And it's never coming back.

It's a terrible feeling. One moment you think you're making film history. Suddenly the AD looks at her watch and the matrix shifts. Whatever the reason there comes a time in many an afternoon when it gets real clear real fast: you're not going to finish your day at this pace. What do you do now?

Stuff You Can't Get Blamed For

On one picture I did, a lamp operator left a fixture too close to a sprinkler system head while we went for lunch. By the time we got back there was a foot of water covering the entire set. To a director that's *force majeur*. The insurance covered the cost of cleaning and the overtime. It wasn't the director's fault.

How about if the dolly breaks down during a complicated shot and we lose two hours getting a replacement? Technically it's not the director's fault. But the shot could have been changed. It could have been shot on sticks or with the Steadicam. It wouldn't have had the aesthetic appeal the director was going for perhaps. But while the delay isn't technically the director's fault maybe not everyone is going to see it that way.

Inevitably, the director must face this question: Should I rush and risk spoiling my day's work? Or should I hold the course and plunge the unit into expensive overtime?

Playing Catch-up

The first job is to perform the calculations. Based on how quickly the unit has worked in the past it's easy to calculate how much work they're capable of. If the unit does three set-ups an hour, and there are three hours left in regulation that's nine set-ups. If you need another twelve set-ups your situation is pretty clear. Reduce your shot list or go into overtime. It's like the NASA guys trying to get the Apollo 13 crew home with 13 amps and a roll of duct tape.

Don't just stand there. First do something fast. Cancel the complicated shot. Do a simple master to get as far as you can. While that's getting built make a plan to simplify the remaining work.

The One-er. Short scenes can often be shot in a one-er. One shot with no coverage. If there's little dialogue and what there is works well, one-shot scenes can speed up the process considerably.

Two Position Blocking. Instead of blocking the master with everyone's face more or less open to camera, choose to have one or more of the cast plant themselves with their backs to camera. This accomplishes two things: 1) The B camera gets an over the shoulder close-up simultaneously with the A cam master.; and 2) All we owe is one turn around set-up to get the back to camera close-ups. We just saved an entire setup. That puts us twenty minutes further ahead than we were a minute ago.

Block Shooting. Although unattractive it can save a tremendous amount of time. I refer to the practice of shooting everything in the location that faces the same direction, one after another, regardless of how many scenes are involved. This saves the time turning around to re-light.

The Steadicam. It's a director's article of faith that you can shoot your way out of trouble with the Steadicam. The logic of this is, to hell with the look. We're in so much trouble we'd shoot it with Mom's handycam if we had to. The problem with scenes finished this way is that they look different. Different worse. It's better to realize we're in trouble before it gets this bad. But if one is down to the lemons of thirty minutes until dark, get creative. Mount up and make lemonade.

OVERTIME

I had a show not long ago where the line producer came to me midway through an impossible night and said I absolutely had to wrap on time. He said there were location restrictions. If we didn't wrap we'd be in a serious breach of our agreement. We'd be in a world of trouble with the locals. Overtime (O.T.) was flat out impossible.

I called the LM, with whom I had developed a good working relationship in prep. I asked him if O.T. was forbidden by location rules. He just smiled and rubbed his fingers together. It was about money. I went into overtime and finished the night under considerable stress. I learned months later that the show had come in well under budget.

Most shows go into overtime once in a while. Some less, some more. The best time to discuss O.T. is in prep during scheduling. If the schedule calls for more on any one shooting day than you feel you can do, you must let the producers know that an O.T. situation is likely on that day. This is key. Serve notice that you are concerned that the quality of the filmed material shot that day could be seriously compromised because of time pressure. So when the heat is on in the last few hours the producer is less inclined to get pushy.

Why would a producer get pushy? Because O.T. costs money. A lot of money. It disrupts the schedule. Suddenly everyone's call time has to be pushed for the next day. And now you're running out of light for *tomorrow*. So the pressure goes up. Leaders are judged by their grace under fire. The second you step into O.T. you're under fire.

This means overtime

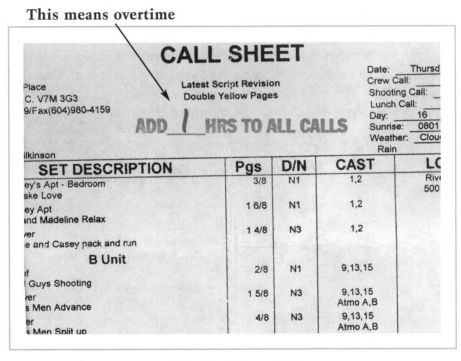

Typical call sheet detail

The pressure comes at you from various places. Obviously there's the financial pressure coming at you from the line producer. There may also be pressure from the crew who can sometimes make it pretty clear they are not happy about working late. An actor may need to catch a plane. You yourself may feel personal pressure from a previously made family commitment, a date, just plain weariness.

Fight the Pressure

Ignore it. Insulate yourself from it. Focus on the shots you need to create the scene. Tell the story.

It also doesn't hurt to acknowledge that these are unusual circumstances. That you are aware of the pressure. That you do not take it lightly. In O.T. I always ask the producer what increments we're working in. In some jurisdictions the unions give a producer very small increments of time. Sometimes 15-minute blocks. In other jurisdictions the units are half hour or one hour minimums. If there's an hour minimum it makes no sense to rush to finish in a half hour. Likewise if the increments are fifteen minutes, a few minutes one way or the other can be important.

Banking Time

Say the O.T. comes in half-hour increments. Say you only need ten minutes to get the shot. It's always worth asking the PM if you can "bank" the time. Most jurisdictions don't allow banking. Even in regular time if the day wraps an hour early the crew is on a flat rate. No savings. But... crews remember. When a crew believes the director has done them a good turn, they will reciprocate. Maybe by extending the "grace" period you need to get a take before lunch. Maybe by letting you run five or ten minutes over without calling it O.T.

The Overtime Bottom Line

Based on how severe you perceive the crisis to be you make a new plan. You pare your shot list down to the minimum number of shots you need to tell the story in keeping with the tone of the show. You present your plan. Then you stick to your guns.

Because there is one thing the working director has to remember about overtime. The line producer may say how much trouble the budget is in. She may promise she'll make it up to you. She may beg and plead. But if you rush to finish and turn in sub-standard work...

No one will thank you.

You alone will take the blame.

Too Tired For Safety

My first major car chase. Two hours into O.T. We were pushing hard. Everyone was bone tired. The grips were racing to take the ancient beater Mercedes chase car down off the camera trailer where we'd been shooting dialogue and gunfire. They slapped the wheels back on the car, unchained it and rolled it off the trailer. The operator, the stunt driver and I bailed in with a camera. We accelerated up to 50 mph or so on our police-controlled, traffic-free, riverside, midnight road. We shot some excellent high speed over-the-hood driver POV. When we arrived back at the set a grip took me quietly aside, white faced and shaking. He pointed at one of our wheels. Four of the five lug nuts — the nuts that hold the wheel on the car — were *missing*....

THE ABBY

There's a prolific AD who became known throughout the industry for a practice he was said to have engaged in frequently. As the story goes, towards wrap time Abby Singer would often call for just one more shot. The director would think of something else. Mr. Singer would then call for just one more shot. Amusing as this may be, the humor can fade late at night when everyone just wants to go home. You'd be amazed how fast the indecisive director can become an Ed Wood.

So what does it mean when the AD announces on set that this is the Abby Singer? It's the second last shot of the day.

The Window Shot

As in, *"Win do we get to go home?"* Seriously. When the director advises the AD that this is the last shot of the day, the AD announces to the crew that this is the window shot. This sets in motion a rush of off-set activity that various departments must do before they go home. But imagine how impressed the crew is going to be if their window turns out to be an Abby. So...

That's a Wrap

That's it. Thank the actors. Shake hands with the keys. Off you go. One down, however many more to go.

Remote filming actor R.H. Thomson under large wind machine
Tina Schliessler Photo

chapter FIVE
THE BIG PICTURE

MENTAL FATIGUE

It's 11 p.m. on a Friday of the sixth week of shooting. You're two hours into overtime. The cast and crew just want to go home. You tell your AD this is the window shot. A surge of relief washes over the unit. Out of the blue the producer shows up with some suggestions for three or four pick-up shots someone at the studio has asked for. Inserts, reaction shots, rib shots (the filmmaker digging the audience in the ribs and saying *"get it?"*). And suddenly it all hits the fan. From some deep well a great blast of anger and frustration suddenly erupts. Your heart rate accelerates, your face reddens, your mouth opens to tell him to go to h...

Let's freeze time right there.

You're *tired*. He's tired. You're all tired. Tired people have shortened tempers. It's science. You've been averaging five hours of sleep per night for the past six weeks. The crew's been getting more but they live harder too so it evens out. This means that you are all much more likely to react in anger for reasons you would find non-angering when you're adequately rested.

Let's flash forward now. It's one year later. The picture came out. It did okay. You suspect that the producer has never quite forgiven you for getting angry that night over the shots he wanted. In any case he hasn't hired you for any of his current shows. The phone is maddeningly silent. Your memory starts to do one of those shadowy transitions, back to a night just one year ago. There's the producer standing in front of you with a list of pick-up shots he wants. Your heart rate is accelerating. Your face is red. Your mouth drops open and you say, *"Why don't you just go to... have a cup of coffee while we shoot those for you."*

My Mind is on the Blink

Tired is the worst possible state to be in when making decisions that could impact your future. So don't. Tell yourself to breathe in and breathe out. Calm blue ocean. There will be plenty of time later to get angry if you still want to. The first casualty of weariness is *judgment*.

Is there anything a director can do about the mind-numbing weariness that comes with the job? Yes there is. Anything that promotes rest is good. Get as much sleep as you can. Eat small nutritious meals. Don't eat a big lunch on set. Don't party too much on the weekends. Don't drink excessively. Laughter is good. So is yoga. Meditation works very well. Fifteen minutes twice a day plus short top-ups when you're tired. The basic premise is that even when your body is at rest, if your mind is racing you will stay weary. But if you can focus your mind on one meaningless word it causes the rest of the jabber and tension to ease away.

United We Stand

Being tired on set is something that happens to everyone. But it's something few want to admit. It's a sign of weakness. This is another case where building human relationships with your co-workers can make the difference between getting the day or going down in flames.

I've learned to recognize the signs in myself. When I begin to feel irritated I always stop and see if it's due to tiredness. If so, I'll tell the AD, the DP, the script supervisor, *"Hey, I'm getting tired, are you?"* Usually that degree of honesty provokes an honest answer. And it encourages us to ignore the petty irritations, pitch in, get something simple and beautiful, and go home.

The flat-out best method of driving away weariness-induced irritation: visualize yourself wearing a suit, working in an office....

THIS TOO SHALL END

When you're in the midst of a shoot it's hard to imagine not being in production. It's so all-consuming you rarely reflect that in a few days or weeks you're going to be sleeping in. But you will be. Unless you hop directly onto another show. Which is great from a career POV. Not quite so great from a personal POV.

The Note On the Fridge

Pick a couple of big directors from a few decades ago. Blockbuster "A" types. Someone you haven't heard of for a while. Want to know where they are now? Many are retired and doubtless living well. But the odds are that a fair number of them are in expensive houses on the beach in Malibu with a nice car, golf clubs, a handful of friends, no kids, no grandkids, no partner, pretty much alone with their golden statuettes. Sound like someone you want to be?

One of the best things about being a working director is the time off. Because shows usually don't happen back to back. Because the pay is usually high enough to eke out a careful existence without working non-stop, there's often a lot of time to spend building a life. A director I know well once told me, *"When I direct a movie it's old news in two or three years. But my kids keep getting better and better over a lifetime."*

Charles with his two sons on Astral Pictures Max
Kharen Hill Photo

Features and episodics are the worst home wreckers. And it's not just the director's problem. The entire cast and crew suffers. We spend all our waking hours for months on end bonding with a group of attractive friends, digging deep in emotional terrain to create something beautiful. How relevant are our partners or our kids going to seem? How long do you think they'll take this?

But...

You have to keep working. Say no too many times or even once to the right project and your career can nosedive.

The reason I'm talking about this here is that your current job is often where your next job comes from. A working director gets more work. People see your name on one thing and they think, *"Hmmm, she must be good. She's directing."* Don't wait too long to trade on this. As mentioned earlier, unless your current show wins an Oscar or an Emmy you are probably more hirable *before* the show wraps than after it plays.

WHY ISN'T YOUR AGENT CALLING?

Your agent needs to be beating the bushes for work *now*. It's important to talk to your agent when you're shooting. Most agents would deny that when you're working they feel less pressure to keep you serviced. But it's a fact of life. I don't mean they ignore you when you're working. They just feel slightly less pressure to sell you than some other director they rep who has promise but is about to go stale. And slightly more or less pressure is often the difference between getting the next job or not.

Changing Lanes

But what if you're directing a syndicated series, action drama. Let's say something in space. Say you feel you belong in features. Here's the quicksand: if you stay too long anywhere, *that's* where you get stuck. How much feature heat does a director with fifteen episodes of *Space Jocks* generate? Think a studio exec is going to say, *"We need a good, solid, reliable director for our 200 million space drama. Hey, let's get that director with fifteen episodes of Space Jocks."* Uh huh. Know who's got a real chance? The guy with one Madonna music video to his credit or a cool commercial for Audi.

You can't stay too long in a place you don't want to be. If features is where you think you should be then do one episode. Maybe a couple. Don't buy that Porsche. Save the money to carry you through the time off you're going to take to direct a no-budget show with Sundance potential. Steve Lamare, a good filmmaker friend/neighbor of mine, refers to this concept as *"self unemployment."*

These are some of the hardest choices the working director will face. The conflict between career, money, lifestyle and family has no easy answers. Every job you take or pass on is a crap shoot. And we all like to believe we're on a path. Not a treadmill.

THE WRAP

Finally the last week of shooting approaches. The last day. Then the last hour. It suddenly becomes clear that this is all going to end. The end of shooting is a lot like the end of a transatlantic flight. Suddenly a tremor goes through the plane. The cabin attendants bustle about collecting headsets. Everyone starts preparing for re-entry to life on the ground.

On a film set it's ushered in by a wave of cell phones ringing. Suddenly everyone is on the phone in their spare moments. Hustling the next job. Snatches of overheard conversations about how many weeks, such and such a location, so and so a star, this studio, that network. Keys offer work to their people. Or not. Actors call agents. Have they heard so and so is shooting such and such?

For the director this flurry of activity can feel a bit like treason. We're still working on this show, right? And then there's the card exchanging, number giving, promises of "we'll get together." All told it's kind of like the last day of camp. *"We'll always be friends, call me as soon as you get home..."* And like the promises kids make on that last day at camp the promises movie people make to stay in contact are really hard to keep.

You know how guilty everyone on the set feels about ignoring their families while they work on this show? Well, they're all about to go on to other shows where they will again feel guilty about ignoring their families. Plus now they'll feel guilty about ignoring all the friends they made on this show. Set relationships fade. Just like summer camp friends. But there's always next summer. One of the best things about remaining in this business for a while is that if you stick around long enough you'll get to be with these people again and again.

One practical note is to keep the cast and crew lists. You often forget the names but you'll always remember there was a great sound person on such and such a show.

Celebrate

"That's a wrap." The last shot of any picture is usually an emotional moment. Whether the show was a good experience or a bad one the last shot means a lot. It means you've gotten through it.

For the director it's especially thought provoking. Wrapping means saying goodbye to a group of people you've grown very close to. It means saying goodbye to the make-believe world you've all been creating and living in. And it means saying goodbye (however temporarily) to the creative power a director has. It means going home to whatever is waiting there. It means unthinkingly saying to your partner, *"Could I get a coffee?"* And your partner responds, *"What, do I look like Craft Service?"*

THE WRAP PARTY
Go. You owe it to the unit, to the picture, to yourself. Besides, wrap parties are a lot of fun. They're a way of getting closure with these people. It's like this giant decompression chamber. The director walks in the door as "the director" and walks out a human being again.

I'm assuming you're a popular director. If you aren't, consider giving the wrap party a pass. There was a director who was very unpopular with the crew on a show in the midwest one winter. A grip warned the director not to come to the wrap party. He did anyway. The crew buried him up to his neck in a snow bank and left him there for a good long while. This was the same director whose car was filled with rotting fish by the transport department at a summer shoot wrap. Dude, I think they're trying to tell you something.

People do surprising things at wrap parties. Mostly good things. They can relax now. They're not auditioning for the job. It's over. Suddenly the 2nd AD is up on the stage singing with the band and he's good. The most unlikely people can dance. And it's always startling to see a team of people you've never seen out of work clothing suddenly appear in dresses and makeup (especially the grips).

For the director the wrap party is a weird mix of feelings. Your entire focus for months on end has been getting the shot, the scene, the performance. Now that's all done. Whatever the show is going to be, the major part of it has ceased being hypothetical. It really is carved in stone now. You wonder, everyone wonders what it's going to be like. You know a lot more about the movie than anyone else. But you don't really know the one thing everybody wants to know: Is it going to be any good?

And at the wrap party there's that unavoidable question, *"What are you doing next?"* Like it's some kind of measure of your ultimate worth. Are you going on to bigger and better or more of the same or unemployment? For the director it's especially hard because most crew people work a lot more than most directors. So frequently they'll all have jobs lined up and you've got postproduction on this. And then god knows what.

What's a good way to characterize how a director feels at a wrap party? It's triumphant, yes. The job has been done. Often against serious odds. But it's also about loss. Something great is over. An older director I respect very much advised me to attend the wrap party as the *father of the bride*. You had a big role in making this day possible. But the wrap party, like a wedding, is to celebrate something *a lot* of people have made possible. And like a wedding it's about the past wishing the future well.

So celebrate the achievement. Wish everyone well. Let it go. Everyone else is winging their way home or on to the next job. But you're headed for the cutting room.

Rigging up to shoot travelling shots on Astral Pictures *Max Kharen Hill Photo*

chapter ## SIX POSTPRODUCTION

THE POST PROCESS

The postproduction process functions differently on different shows but there are enough common practices that it's possible to generalize. The editor assembles and edits the filmed material as it comes in. Ultimately they produce what is called the "editor's cut." Once shooting ends the director sits with the editor producing a "director's cut." Then unless the director has final cut rights in their contract (very rare), the producer screens the cut. Often they accept it as is. Sometimes they will ask for (or simply make) changes. The picture is finally "locked." The sound is edited. The music is composed and recorded. The soundtrack is created and mixed. The colors are corrected. The titles are put on and it's released.

For the director, post is a radical change of gears. You've just come from a noisy set where you had a hundred people coming at you from every direction with a million things all at once. Here in the editing room it's quiet. One on one. Just you and the editor. Postproduction is a lot more technical than production because mechanization is much more prevalent in post. All of the machines have names, specific functions, and are capable of an almost infinite variety of creative effects.

The problem for the director in post is in knowing what you want, knowing what you're likely to get, knowing how and when to ask for it. The process is flexible but it's inherently linear. In other words the process likes to build B on A, C on B and so forth down the line. So although the bad color timing on an otherwise useable shot may irritate the director, if you make the editor stop picture cutting to fiddle with color balance you waste valuable time.

And time is again the director's arch enemy. There's a post schedule. There's an "air date" or a "release date." There's rarely sufficient time to explore all of the possibilities in the footage you've shot. So the director's key to post becomes understanding the process. In order to direct it as effectively as the shooting.

THE CUTTING ROOM
The "Cutting Room" has a magical sound. And magic does happen there. But the physical reality is anything but. It's usually a small windowless room with a desktop computer, a few drives and a monitor or two. There are two or three chairs, some shelves for tapes, maybe a couple of call sheets pinned to the wall. Glamorous it isn't.

Here's how the production chain works: You shoot footage on set during production. If it's film it goes to the lab. They process the dailies, strike a workprint if it's a pure film finish (increasingly rare), or transfer into the digital medium. Then the tapes go to the edit facility where an assistant digitizes (records) the dailies into the computer hard drive. Somewhere along the line copies of these dailies are made for the producers, director, DP, etc. The editing systems vary and change but what they all do is store the shots in folders organized by scene. The editor then begins to assemble those shots into edited scenes and the edited scenes into a completed show.

Say the director's shooting style was to shoot every scene in one long, continuous, uncuttable take. All the editor has to do is cut the slate off the head of the shot, cut off the tail run-out (after you've said "cut"), and join all the shots together. But most directors shoot coverage. So the editor assembles all the shots, cutting to and from masters, close-ups, inserts, in much the same way that you would organize a document with a word processor. Cutting, moving, pasting, deleting.

The computer-based editing systems can perform a wide variety of visual and audio effects. The software is able to fade, dissolve, speed ramp, do fast and slow motion, color correct, add titles, modify the sound for volume and equalization. It can also perform interesting visual effects. Photoshop-like stuff. But the editor is usually far too busy to play with that. They leave everything but the actual picture cutting to specialists. The editor concentrates on cutting the story.

What Exactly Is an Editor?

Forget the images Hollywood gives us of a humble clerk huddled over a Moviola obediently gluing the director's shots together and nodding admiringly at every insight that drops from the director's lips. Think instead of Perry White. You know the hard bitten, tough as nails newspaper editor that Clark Kent/Superman works for. Perry shouts and raves. He takes Lois Lane's promising but disorganized story copy and *edits it*. Sometimes he even *rewrites* it into something he feels people will understand and respond to. A good film editor doesn't usually rave or smoke cigars but the newspaper analogy holds. A film editor doesn't simply join shots together. *He creates a living, breathing story out of the elements he's given.* Sometimes with help from the director. Sometimes not. The editor is a storyteller. On the same level with the writer and the DP.

During the entire time the director was shooting the picture the editor was cutting the material as it came in. He may also cut problem scenes together for the director from time to time. Plus check things for the producer. Editors typically spend 12 – 16 hours a day at the keyboard. They generally don't get paid overtime. Editors experience eye strain, carpal tunnel syndrome, posture and weight problems. It's not particularly healthy work.

Editors work at different speeds on different types of shows. In episodic TV and on TV movies it is not uncommon for the editor to have a pretty good cut ready a few days after wrap. On features there is generally a lot more time to explore the possibilities so the pace is slower.

In any event, the director usually calls the editor a few days prior to wrapping the show and sets up a time to come in and start work on the director's cut. The editor usually wants some time to get his cut in order so he has something presentable to show the director. He will often send a tape of this assembly to the director a day or two prior to their arrival so the director can make notes.

THE DIRECTOR IN THE CUTTING ROOM
When the director arrives for work in the cutting room the editor will usually screen the entire show for the director. They'll talk, agree on a plan of action, then get to work. The

editor sits at the keyboard touching the controls. The director sits behind the editor. Watching, commenting, directing.

Every editor has their own procedure. It's worth paying very close attention to get a sense of how each individual works. Editors tend to cut for *meaning* first. Because if the scene doesn't tell the story there's no story. So as the meaning gradually becomes clear over the course of the editing process, the editor tends to focus more and more on the *feel.*

One very common cutting technique that can confuse inexperienced directors is the "sound first" style many editors use to cut a dialogue scene that has a lot of overlaps. They'll first cut the audio together to form a rational-sounding conversation. Then they'll put the right pictures with it. Until the moment the procedure is completed it all looks like gibberish to the uninformed.

A director who understands the process will know enough to wait for the editor to finish before commenting. But sometimes it's hard to know if he's finished. He's sitting in front of you hunched over his keyboard tapping away. The picture starts to run. Is that it? Am I supposed to say something now?

When I worked as an editor I remember directors saying, *"Let's go to close-up a beat earlier."* I would make the cut. I'd preview it once and see it needed a few frames trimmed. But the director would go, *"Nah, doesn't work. Let's try...."* So what am I as an editor supposed to do? Agree with my director and move on? Even though I know the right thing to do is adjust the cut? Or should I stop and argue? Try not to put your editor in this position.

What Editors Hate

There's a behavior directors sometimes exhibit in the cutting room that drives most editors crazy. The director will be watching a shot then leap up and point at (even touch!) the screen and shout, "Cut *there!*"

Dude, editors know how to cut from a wide shot to a close-up. It's what they do. Editors don't need schooling from a director on how to make a dissolve or an overlap. Appropriate comments are things like, *"That feels a little slow"* or *"Try cutting the coverage with more dialogue overlaps"* or *"I'd like to stay in the master quite a bit longer."* An editor will take a request like that and implement it. Without you telling him which buttons to hit.

Which raises another sore point for editors. Don't touch the machine. Keep your fingers off the buttons. Some editors are comfortable with a director taking a scene away and cutting it themselves. If they have the extra equipment and don't feel offended or threatened by this it's often great for a director to work this way. But feel it out carefully before you ask. You're going to be in this room with this person for a while.

EDITING FIXES

Say there are problems in the area of meaning. If a particular story beat is not coming across clearly, the director has a variety of tools. Reshooting is best. But very few shows have the budget to bring actors and crews back. A much less expensive insert shot will often help, if there's budget for any 2nd unit or insert unit shooting during post. Always ask the editor to insert a "scene missing" card if a pick-up shot is planned. Otherwise you could grow so used to looking at it without the card that you'll gradually stop being aware of how badly you need the additional shot. Plus a (by now) cash-strapped producer just might say, *"Works fine for me. We don't need it."*

An off-camera line of dialogue can often work wonders to get a story beat across. And if you're bringing cast back later for ADR anyway it's a "free" solution. But during editing it's important that you sell the idea of adding a line. Again there are two ways of doing this: 1) Tell everybody; 2) Show everybody by recording the line. The latter method tends to work best.

Tell the editor you want to record some off-camera lines. He'll ask his assistant to have a mike standing by. You can read the line yourself (or ask a handy member of the opposite sex if appropriate). Put some effort into it. Get into character. Mimic the voice you need. It's fun. It works.

Script Changes in Post

The editor will sometimes take one look at a scene and say, *"This doesn't work,"* then cut it the way you argued in prep to have it written. It's remarkable how pragmatic everyone gets about script changes in post. Often when the director asks for script changes during prep it's called *"artistic differences."* When an editor arbitrarily reworks large pieces of unclear material it's called *"saving the picture."*

Much of the work in editing revolves around removing redundant stuff. Audiences are smart. If you beat them over the head they lose interest fast. The director's role in postproduction story editing usually begins with the words *"what if...."* And it's usually what if we cut from this line to that one and throw out everything in between.

The House of Cards

Editors in the days of film used to get very defensive over their cut. In a way they had to. They were cutting actual film. If a director wanted to try it a thousand ways the film strip itself would turn into an "accordion." It would click and flip going through the gate of the Moviola. They'd have to order reprints. It got expensive and very time consuming. Frank Irvine, the wonderful old-school editor of *The Grey Fox*, used to say *"It's a house of cards. I won't change a frame."* (This from a guy who took a novice director's first and only two-hour feature, cut it down to twenty-four minutes and said something to the effect, *"The rest is dreck."* He got his way too.)

Assistant Will Waring with editor Frank Irvine CFE on My Kind of Town
Charles Wilkinson Photo

Now that editing is "nonlinear" digital there's no limit to the number of cuts and versions an editor can make. But some editors still buy into the "house of cards" thing. Sometimes they're right. Sometimes they're being lazy. But as a director you have a right to see the material cut together as you intended. The editor has the obligation to show you. If it doesn't work you'll see that.

It's In Your Contract and It Isn't

Director's Guild contracts all have language setting forth the director's rights during editing. And each individual director signs a deal memo that specifies how many weeks you are expected to work in post. There's also language that limits the director's rights. What it boils down to is this: Make the picture work great within the time you have. That's all a working director can do. Regardless of all the careful thought you've put into the prep and all the sweat you've put into the shooting, the day you deliver your cut the producers can cut in dancing girls if they want. This is one of the biggest reasons directors aspire to the ultimate control that comes with "A" status. It's just so heart-wrenching to see someone strangling your baby.

This is yet another example of how important it is to develop a good working relationship with the team, in this case the producer and the editor. They want the show to be good and people are hesitant to argue with their friends. But at a certain point the director has to trust the process. Your director's cut gets sent out to all the execs who have approval at the studio/network. If the producer takes over and really ruins the show it's not like the studio execs won't remember your cut.

And the reality is that most of the producers you work with (like most actors and crew) will be talented, committed individuals.

Temp Music

One great tool you have for making your director's cut work is *temporary music*, temp. Ralph Rosenblum in his must-read book on editing, *When The Shooting Stops The Cutting Starts* talks at length of how his knowledge of music enhanced his abilities as an editor. It's the same with a director.

The editor sometimes just doesn't have time to put good temp music into his cut. A director with a knowledge of music will have been thinking about and gathering temp music for this particular show since his first reading of the script.

A great place to look for temp music is on soundtracks from existing films. Many modern films release soundtrack CDs complete with underscoring, action scenes, love themes, everything. These make wonderful dinner music to play at home. When the director needs a track that says "modern dysfunctional youth joy riding through the slums" you'll reach into your collection for Stewart Copeland's amazing track from Francis Copolla's *Rumblefish*.

DIRECTING MUSIC

There are two basic kinds of film music. When Tom Cruise sings along with Tom Petty's "Free Fallin'" in *Jerry Maguire*, that's what most people think of when you say film music. But that's only a small part of what film music is. The main part is called the *score*: the underscoring, the themes, the scary cues, the action cues. The *"da duh, da duh, da duh"* cue from *Jaws*. That's scoring.

High-budget shows hire well-known composers to create the score. And they buy popular songs. High-budget shows frequently spend more on music than the average indy film's entire budget.

Smaller budget shows simply can't afford popular songs. And most indy shows have no place for pop songs. Imagine *Sexy Beast* with a Britney Spears single in it... But virtually all shows have some form of scoring. And for that you need a composer.

Music is an enormously powerful tool in the director's box. Music is second only to performance and camera for expressing emotion and creating mood. The director should always be on the lookout for musical ideas during shooting. Does the story's teenage kid have a rock band, however bad? Record them. Is the story a modern street drama set in Little Italy? How about blending mandolins with modern electrics? Is there a factory that figures prominently in your story? Are there rhythmic sounds the machines make? Ask the producer to have the sound mixer spend an hour recording the machines. A composer can make anything into music. Chains rattling on pipes can be a beautiful sound when taken out of context.

Choosing the Composer

In many cases on long-form productions the producer will invite the director to have input into choosing the composer. The producer and director will ask a number of composers whose work they know, composers who are available and can work at that budget level. You'll send them a script and invite them to audition. They play samples. They talk about what they hear for style, instrumentation, etc. Ultimately the composer who seems to have the most promising approach to the show is hired. The director works with her and a score is produced.

As director you should always keep in mind that you can go to a composer with a problem. Say the attraction between the two leads is not instantly obvious, but it needs to be. A talented composer can create the illusion that two people on opposite sides of the room are falling in love. Same thing with action scenes that need help. How scary would the *Psycho* shower scene be if instead of using Bernard Herrman's terrifying score, Hitchcock had gone with the Bee Gees? When a composer works with the director as part of the storytelling team amazing things can happen.

Not Choosing the Composer

But often the working director has no input in that decision. Sometimes the producer has a relationship with a composer who can deliver adequate music on time on budget. To the director it's less than ideal to have a composer whose number one goal is simply to get the producer's next show.

But there are ways of working within a shotgun marriage like this. If the composer is working for the producer and the producer has great musical taste, no problem. If the producer has less than great taste look at it from the composer's POV. All musicians love music. They don't get paid enough to do it for the money. So if they're working for a producer who says, "Just put some sweet stuff here and some scary stuff there," how engaged will the composer be? Any composer worth anything would much rather work for/with people who appreciate the process and push hard for excellence. And keep in mind that the composer can't be sure you're not the next "A" director. They want to work with you.

What Composers Hate

Composers tend to hate temp music. Directors put in these wonderful temp cues: rich, fully orchestrated pieces from *The Fugitive*, which everyone loves. Then the composer has to try to reproduce that with 5% of the music budget James Newton Howard had. And suddenly everyone thinks the composer is lame.

Obviously a director should use temp music of a magnitude that the show can afford. If there's only $20,000 in the entire music budget don't use temp from *The English Patient*. There are lots of musical styles that aren't expensive. The most common and least interesting is the synth score. Lower budget producers often use the synth score as an inexpensive substitute for orchestration. But live jazz groups aren't expensive. Neither is piano or string quartet. The local symphony is often available at a very reasonable price.

For songs there are always emerging groups that need a movie credit. They'll give sync rights to their songs for little or nothing. And your show gets a hip, alternative feel.

Time Pressure — Again

It's a rule of thumb that the sooner the composer can give you something to listen to, the more likely you'll get something that works. The problem for the composer is *picture changes*.

If you had all the time in the world the composer would wait until the picture was completely edited before starting the

music. That way, when the girl takes the boy's hand the composer can play a little flourish. The cue plays on, girl kisses
boy and there's a crescendo. And it's all in perfect sync. This
kind of work takes time. But if the composer scores this scene
and then the scene is re-cut, the composer has to go back and
edit or recompose so everything fits again. Music editing is
way more complex than picture editing.

DIRECTING THE SOUND MIX

The sound mix creates a sound track for your film that has
clear and understandable dialogue, exciting sound effects,
stirring music. All balanced perfectly. It also has the power to
create and maintain the mood.

And if you thought picture editing was complex wait until
you sit in a large mixing studio. Typically it has a mixing console that stretches 20 – 30 feet long. On it, under it, beside it,
and behind it are an array of high tech components that make
a 747 cockpit look like a pocket calculator.

Mixing console at dbc sound
Otis Photo

What is a Mix?

This is a complex topic, but the director needs to acquire a certain amount of technical understanding of the mix in order to direct it effectively. Mix studios charge anywhere from a few hundred to a few thousand dollars an hour. The sound mix on a long form can take anywhere from two weeks to two months. So it's obvious the director can't simply sit there and say, *"I don't like that sound, change it."*

Simply, a sound mix is where everything an audience needs to hear in a movie is blended together to express meaning and mood. Typically there is a lead mixer with two mixers working under him. The lead mixer usually has responsibility for mixing all the dialogue. The other two deal with music and sound effects.

They sit at the mixing console, also called the "board," and manipulate the faders up and down to make sounds louder and quieter. They twist dials to add or subtract reverb, EQ, and various other types of effects. And they occasionally connect other "outboard" pieces of gear to filter out unwanted noise.

A Million Tracks

Why do the mixers have all those individual faders? Each fader represents one track of audio. To grossly oversimplify, say all of a certain actor's dialogue for the wide shots is on faders number 1 and 2. The dialogue for medium shots is on faders 3 and 4. The close-ups are faders 5 and 6. In this way the mixer can balance the levels, the EQ, the reverb, so as to maintain the illusion that the scene happened within real time. Not over the course of a long day with airplanes flying over one minute and not the next, heavy traffic during rush hour and so on.

Add to this several tracks for any ADR that might have been recorded for the particular actor. Then multiply this times the number of actors in any given scene. *That's* why so many faders. And that's just for dialogue. Add to that as many as fifty sound effects tracks, twenty or more music tracks. It adds up.

The Director Preps For the Mix

During the later stages of picture editing, the sound editing team assembles and starts their work. The dialogue editor will assess the location-recorded production track, check out alternate takes, make a list of ADR she thinks is required.

The sound effects (SFX) editor will do the same with the sound effects. He generates lists of what can be sourced from FX collections, what needs to be recorded in the field, and what the Foley team can handle. And there will be a music spotting screening with the composer. In this screening decisions will be made about where music is needed and what it needs to accomplish.

Obviously, much of the prep work is of a routine technical nature and there's little need for director input. In fact if the director never talks to any of the sound editors and doesn't bother going to the mix, the editors and mixers are more than capable of making the show sound perfectly adequate. It's when the director wishes for something unusual that conversation with these people is needed.

Say the director has strong feelings about specific sound effects. Now is the time to let the head SFX editor know. If the sounds aren't recorded and placed on tracks for the mixer they won't be in the show. And just as you avoided giving dumb directions to the picture editor, you really need to avoid wasting the sound editor's time with comments like, *"Okay, when the bad guy shoots — his gun should make a really loud bang...."*

These people are good. They've done this a million times before. A good rule is: If you want your show to sound pretty much like other shows in the genre, relax. That's what the sound people will give you. But if you want something unusual, you have to tell them.

THE PRE MIX

Once the sound editors have finished editing all of their various production dialogue, ADR, Foley, Sound FX, Ambiance and so on, they hand it over (generally in a digital format on one or more hard drives) to the mixing team. By this point it may be that the picture has been color timed and corrected. It may be that the visual effects have been finished and edited in. Sometimes even the titles and credits are done. So the sound mixers will be mixing to an otherwise completed film. The significance of this will become clear in a moment.

The mixing team needs to do a tremendous amount of purely routine work before the really creative part of the mix can happen. This is called the pre-mix. And the director and producers rarely attend all of this. Why not?

Take the dialogue for example. All the dialogue for any given scene must be adjusted for volume, EQ, and especially background noise such that if you were to play the dialogue alone without any other added sounds it would sound entirely natural. In other words, although the background noise levels and mike placement may have been radically different between the master shot and the close-ups (where typically the mike can be placed closer, thus reducing background noise), each individual and often different sounding shot must be adjusted, filtered, noise reduced, turned up or down until the entire scene sounds as smooth, clean, and seamless as the budget can afford.

In general the pre-mix sees the mixing team taking the often hundreds of tracks and pre-mixing them down into a manageable number of tracks. So that later in the mix when the director says, *"The dialogue in this scene is a little too quiet,"* the mixer can simply raise the overall level of the dialogue without having to adjust every single track.

Virtually all film mixing boards are computerized and automated. So when the effects mixer slowly raises the volume of a particular sound effect over the course of a scene the computer "memorizes" it. Every subsequent time the movie reaches that part the actual fader on the mixing console will raise. *All by itself.*

If a director has the time it can be very worthwhile to drop in to the pre-mix and spend an hour or two each day. It helps to develop a working relationship with the mixing team and it familiarizes the director with the problems the mixers are facing. For example, let's say several scenes have borderline dialogue, because the background noise is quite high. If the director happens to be there when these scenes are being pre-mixed it will become clear that the best you can hope for is to make that particular dialogue *adequate*. If you aren't aware of this and you walk into the main mix and hear that dialogue, you'll likely waste hours having the mixers demonstrate why this dialogue can't sound fantastic.

The Mix Begins

The director is offered a chair at a desk above and behind the mixing console and team. In attendance are probably the picture editor, possibly the sound editors, the composer, the producer. The lead mixer usually offers to play back the entire picture, just to give a sense of where things are and how far they need to go. I mentioned earlier that the mixers are often mixing to a pretty much complete picture. Color timed, titles, everything. When they press "play" the picture fades up, the music begins and...

You watch your movie for the first time!

This is the very first time this film has played with proper color, titles, music, effects, and clean dialogue. The impact on a director is often extraordinary.

From the moment you first read the script, this movie has existed in your imagination. One by one each component came into being. First the shooting, then the editing, then music, sound, visual effects, titles. As long as one element remained unfinished the film has remained partially imaginary. Now it's real. This is the show. Everything is there. Adjustments will be made. There will be shifts in emphasis. But if you or anyone in the production team has been deluding themselves about what it is you're making, now is the moment you absolutely cannot avoid confronting the reality of what you have actually made.

Sometimes it's a stunning surprise, a moment of real triumph. Sometimes not. Regardless of your reaction, you're not being paid to watch the show. You're being paid to make it better. Don't let your reaction blind you to the many subtle things you can do to improve it.

THE MIX

So now you've seen/heard it. You have a sense of what the show is. A sense of what it needs. You may have made specific notes about changes you'd like. The most common mix notes usually involve placement of music and relative loudness. It's not uncommon for a piece of music to conflict badly with the dialogue and sound effects. We'll get to that. But first things first.

The mixing team could use some encouragement, *"Nice work folks, you really smoothed out the dialogue, etc."* The lead mixer's position is a difficult one. They require a high degree of artistic and technical skill. They also possess diplomatic skills so finely honed that I sometimes think a good lead mixer could resolve the Middle East conflict in an afternoon. To say that tempers can flare in the mixing studio is an understatement. It's time to get to work.

The mixer presses "play." The projector flickers to life and away we go. The team rolls ahead for anywhere from ten seconds to five minutes. Then they stop and go back to where one of them (or you) had a problem and re-start from that point. In this way they gradually work their way through the show. It's important to remember that the three mixers are not yet permanently blending their work together. The music can be totally wrong and yet the dialogue and effects mixers are happily working away achieving lasting perfection. Remember, the computer learns. It doesn't forget.

You hear something you're not sure of. Your mouth drops open to comment, to bring the team to a halt. Wait. The mixers prefer that you let things go forward for a while to see if it's something they've noticed. Usually it is and they catch it on another pass. If not, speak up. It's very unlikely the team will not have noticed something obviously wrong. But what they may miss are sounds that are supposed to be happening off-screen that have an impact on the on-screen action. Say the sounds of the gallows construction crew outside should be having an impact on the prisoners in their cells. The mixers will often need you to tell them how much of an impact.

A tip: Use the **numbers**. There are time code numbers at the bottom of the screen. They usually measure elapsed time. Each reel starts at the successive hour. Reel 3 time code addresses begin at 3:00:00:00. So the second you notice something that sounds wrong you want to jot the number down on the pad in front of you. Then when they stop, an appropriate way to raise the issue with the mixers is to say, *"The hammering at 5:05 needs to be louder."* They'll tap those numbers onto the pad and you're instantly back there. Conversely, amateurs identify themselves in a mix with comments like *"The hammering back there before Jesse smiles needs to be louder."*

If the director has a radical note, now is exactly the right time to express it. The mixers will work away doing what they consider to be normal-sounding work unless they're told differently. As the director you potentially have enormous power in the mix. Your range of possibilities stretches from dead silence to deafening noise and everything in between. For example, sometimes a director will turn the dialogue down to nothing in a scene. They'll let the music play or the wind blow. It can have an amazing effect.

Likewise, a director can request a sound that isn't there. Say you suddenly realize that what your family dinner conversation scene needs is to remove the dialogue and replace it with the angry squabbling of a flock of penguins. Ask for it. Chances are the mixers have online access to extensive sound effects collections. If not, they'll ask the SFX editor to find one and fly it in. It normally takes only a few moments to deal with such a request.

Music Mixing

Composers hate directors messing around with their music. But sometimes it's necessary. Once I was mixing a long chase scene. The music was pounding rock. After a time it started to grate. I asked the mixer what the track layout for the music was. He told me the guitars, bass, horns, and drums were all on separate tracks. I said, *"Great, pull everything out except the drums at 11:21, let the drums carry us to 11:37, then slam everything back in."* He tried it. It created a welcome respite in the action. Maybe the horn by itself will sound great. And how about drums and bass? Play with it.

Sometimes a music cue will sound completely wrong. It will fight with the dialogue or the FX. Or it will have the wrong tone. It's important to flag these cues right away. Let the composer know (if she's around) and she can start hunting for a solution. Sometimes the composer can remix the cue and bring it back. Other times she can create an entirely new cue. Most often she will suggest "lifting" a cue from earlier or later in the show. Something like, *"There was a great sting of low, ominous underscore in the title overture. Could we just lift that one note?"*

Hide That Flaw

Here's something weird. Most human brains only process one thing at a time. That's the principle magicians live by. Every magic trick takes place under the shadow of a *diversion*. That technique works at least as well in film. Say there's a moment in an actor's performance you hate. Say his eyes accidentally crossed the lens at one point. Tell the sound mixer to place a dog bark or a car start or something a frame or two prior to the offending moment. It doesn't need to be loud. It's amazing how the offending moment simply *disappears*.

Turn It Up

Loudness is relative and there are physical limits to how loud movie sound can be. If you have a very quiet movie, a moderate sound will seem loud. If you have a show with wall to wall gun battles, at a certain point nothing is going to seem loud. What will happen in a mix session with a director or producer who doesn't understand this is that they'll keep telling the mixer to make the music or the effects louder. Which the mixer will do. He'll run the levels right up into the red. Then along comes a scene with a tremendous explosion. The mixer will be told to make that *really* loud. He's already at max. Where's he going to go? The answer is that he has to go back and undo all your requests to turn it up. So that when real volume is called for there'll be some room left.

A tip? Keep your eyes on the meters. They're big, right under the screen. If you see that the needles are spending most of their time near the top, know this: The theatre projectionist and the audience at home will simply turn your show down for you.

Fighting in the Mix

Directors rarely fight with the mix team. The mix team rarely fights with each other. But put two or more people in the room who all share some measure of creative power and the potential for conflict can loom large. As director, by this point in the show you're getting tired of babysitting and consensus building. You're tired of manipulating everyone to stop fighting long enough to do good work. But you have to hang on for just a bit longer. Directors need to exercise all their artistic, technical, and persuasive abilities in the mixing studio.

The sound mix is the last place the director can make real improvements in the picture. After this it's someone else's turn.

Automated faders on the board at dbc sound
Otis Photo

chapter
IT'S OVER

Fade to black. Credits roll. Lights come up. Shake hands with the mixers and the sound editors. Hug the picture editor. Exchange compliments with the composer and the producers. Walk through the door out onto the street and it hits you. It's over. For the *auteur* or "A" director the end of the sound mix is the beginning of a whole new phase. Promotion, festivals, interviews, articles. But for the working director this is often the end of the line.

We frequently have little or no role in what happens after the sound mix. Most shows are not entered in festivals of any kind. Most directors won't be invited to do Leno. Most directors never even make the cover of their own guild newsletter.

It feels *weird*. After so much activity. So many calls. So many questions. And now, nothing. But there are a number of things the working director can and should do after the mix.

Get Copies

There is language in every guild director agreement regarding the director's copy. This is something about which you leaned on your agent during contract negotiations, remember? What you need here is a copy of the show in *digital format*. A digital copy will look great on your reel and won't degrade rapidly.

Thank You Notes

During postproduction it's a good idea to select one of the best production stills you can find from the show. It's a simple matter to photoshop the image into a cool souvenir postcard. You can send this out to the entire cast and crew thanking them for their contribution and advising them that the show is finally finished. It reminds everyone that you valued their work and it keeps people thinking about the show.

Charles and Dennis Weaver on ABC-TV Harvest of Lies
Myrl Coulter Photo

Do a slight revision of the card changing the wording to make it simply an announcement that you've completed a new show. Then send it around to everyone who is in a position to hire you.

Send one out to each of the trade publications. They're always hungry for news of this kind. If they print it people will read your name in a positive context. If you live in a smaller community or even a distinct neighborhood of a large city there are almost always small local papers. They often welcome copy about the arts in the community.

THANK THE MONEY
Send the above postcards to the network/studio/distributors as well. It's been a while since you wrapped. A while since you met face to face. They have other projects they're thinking about directors for. They should be considering you. Which they will the second that postcard hits their desk.

Stay in touch with whoever in the organization has current release date info. Prepare alternate wording for your postcard that you can send around for release/broadcast date to contacts, cast, crew, and friends.

PRODUCER CLOSURE
Take the producer who hired you to lunch. Ask her point blank if she's happy with the show. If she's going to recommend you. If she'd hire you again. If there were simple misunderstandings maybe they can be fixed. Remember what the producer I spoke of earlier said:

> *"Everyone who is not your friend... is your enemy"*

Bad word of mouth can destroy a career. It can build and grow without any real basis in fact. It needs to be dealt with. If you hear or sense that someone is slagging you, talk to them. Usually the person you're concerned about is the producer who hired you. Hence this lunch.

Find out if she has been or is planning to bad-mouth you. Ask her straight out. Ask why. Make an effort to see it from her POV. If the show turned out awful and it's obviously your fault there's not much you can do. But that's usually not the case. Nine times out of ten if producers are angry with a director it's because they feel the director didn't show them the proper respect. They feel the director exceeded their authority. You changed dialogue or adjusted story or went into overtime too often. That sort of thing.

I've known producers to post-lunch re-hire directors they pre-lunch wouldn't have hired to clean their septic tank. It's important to recognize how much history you two have together. How much less likely you will be to fight in the future now that you know each other's signals.

YOU'LL ALWAYS WORK IN THIS TOWN AGAIN
Once in a while a show goes badly. Sometimes lasting enemies are made. When a working director experiences this and then goes through one of the slow spots that happen periodically, it's tempting to think that a few too many bridges have been burned.

If everybody who has been warned they would never work in this town again actually didn't still work here the town would be empty. Most people who bad-mouth are not respected. What kind of a person goes around saying nasty things behind other people's backs? *Everyone* has enemies. I seriously know people who are critical of the Dalai Lama. The trick is not to dwell on it. Keep moving forward. Keep working.

Directing Your Inner Writer

Some working directors spend off-time developing their own screenplays. Industry majors sometimes laugh about this. They say it's like an airline captain who secretly wants to be a cabin attendant. But directors write screenplays because they are storytellers. They write screenplays because it's one of only a few proven ways a working director is ever going to get material that could propel them to the next level. But there are risks. Writing takes months. Months of not chasing directing. If the script doesn't get made, the director has now slipped way back in the pack.

I think some people are born with an extra writing gene. Their work is so brilliant. It seems so effortless. The rest of us have to work very hard to acquire even the most basic skills. Screenwriting is enormously complex. But with some time and effort it's possible to learn how to recognize a good script when you see one. It's possible to learn how to critique a script. To make a bad one less bad and a good one better. There are excellent books on the subject. My personal favorite is Robert McKee's *Story*. If you spend a few months studying McKee's book you may not emerge as a brilliant screenwriter. But what you will definitely acquire is a greatly enhanced ability to recognize what's good and to *fix* what isn't.

Shameless Self-Promotion Time

It's obvious you need to update your reel and resume and get it to your agent immediately. While you're at it talk to your agent. What are you up for? Why not? What can you do? Who can you meet?

Show business operates on buzz. Most people never see most shows but *everyone* feels the buzz. So with the limited resources of a working director on a show you're no longer officially working on, get busy and create some buzz.

Festivals

The show you just finished is almost certainly eligible for a number of film festivals. There are festivals dedicated to infomercials, industrials, weddings and Bar Mitzvah shows. There will definitely be venues for yours. You don't even need to win. Just get accepted. Get *short listed*. If you get rejected from enough festivals even *that* becomes an item: (*"See the film no festival dared to show..."*). Festival activity looks great on your resume.

TAKE A MOMENT

Whether you throw a huge party or hike alone up a mountain, this is a time you need to pause and pat yourself on the head. *You directed a film.* That is truly an achievement to be proud of. Know this: Your family is proud of you. Your friends and acquaintances are proud of you. You have just done something the vast majority of people would give almost anything to do. You did the verb, you get the noun. You directed — you are a director.

Take a moment to reflect on the working director's good fortune. As hard as it is to believe, people are actually paying us to do the most interesting, the most fulfilling, the most absolutely cool job in the world.

Cheers to you for the success you've had. Do something beautiful with the amazing ride in front of you.

God speed.

With a little help from my friends on Disney's Out of Nowhere
Chris Large Photo

About the Author

Charles Wilkinson is a working director with extensive credits in film and television. He lives with his wife and three children in Vancouver.

Kharen Hill Photo

To contact the author, go to:
www.charleswilkinson.com

MICHAEL WIESE PRODUCTIONS

Since 1981, Michael Wiese Productions has been dedicated to providing both novice and seasoned filmmakers with vital information on all aspects of filmmaking. We have published more than 70 books, used in over 500 film schools and countless universities, and by hundreds of thousands of filmmakers worldwide.

Our authors are successful industry professionals who spend innumerable hours writing about the hard stuff: budgeting, financing, directing, marketing, and distribution. They believe that if they share their knowledge and experience with others, more high quality films will be produced.

And that has been our mission, now complemented through our new web-based resources. We invite all readers to visit www.mwp.com to receive free tipsheets and sample chapters, participate in forum discussions, obtain product discounts — and even get the opportunity to receive free books, project consulting, and other services offered by our company.

Our goal is, quite simply, to help you reach your goals. That's why we give our readers the most complete portal for filmmaking knowledge available — in the most convenient manner.

We truly hope that our books and web-based resources will empower you to create enduring films that will last for generations to come.

Let us hear from you at anytime.

Sincerely,
Michael Wiese
Publisher, Filmmaker

www.mwp.com

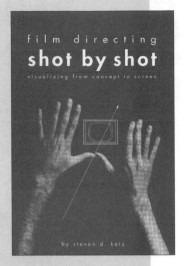

CINEMATIC MOTION
2ND EDITION

STEVEN D. KATZ

BEST SELLER
OVER 30,000 UNITS SOLD!

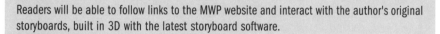

Cinematic Motion has helped directors create a personal camera style and master complex staging challenges for over a decade. In response to the opportunities offered by digital technology, this second edition adds essential chapters on digital visualization and script breakdown.

S. D. Katz uses extensive illustrations to explain how to create extended sequence shots, elaborate moving camera choreography, and tracking shots with multiple story points. Interviews with top Hollywood craftspeople demonstrate how to bring sophisticated ideas to life.

Readers will be able to follow links to the MWP website and interact with the author's original storyboards, built in 3D with the latest storyboard software.

"There are a precious few ways to learn the subtleties of filmmaking and challenges of cinematography: Watch great movies repeatedly; go to a great film school; read Steven D. Katz's Film Directing: Shot by Shot *and* Cinematic Motion. *The practical and pragmatic information is balanced by the insights of great filmmakers, Allen Daviau, Ralph Singleton and John Sayles.* Cinematic Motion *is the definitive workbook for both the aspiring as well as the accomplished filmmaker."*
 — John McIntosh, Chair, Computer Art, School of Visual Arts, NYC

"There are few authors or books that reach 'must-read' status. The works of Steven Katz have achieved this appellation. Cinematic Motion *is a remarkable tutorial for any aspiring or working director. Clear, practical, and wise, the book is an essential guide to understanding and implementing staging for the motion picture medium."*
 — Sam L Grogg, Ph.D., Dean, AFI Conservatory

"In Cinematic Motion, *Katz succeeds in breaking down the daunting tasks that a director faces when choreographing actors and the camera on set."*
 — Dan Ochiva, Millimeter Magazine

STEVEN D. KATZ, who lives in New York City, is an award-winning filmmaker and writer, and the author of *Shot by Shot*, the now classic text on cinematic style and technique.

$27.95 | 362 PAGES | ORDER # 121RLS | ISBN: 0-941188-90-6

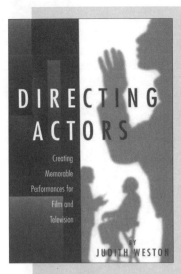

THE FILM DIRECTOR'S INTUITION:
SCRIPT ANALYSIS AND REHEARSAL TECHNIQUES

JUDITH WESTON

The craft of directing is well known to include shot composition and understanding of the technology. But directors need to know how to prepare so that their ideas achieve a level of intuitive truth. This means deep script analysis, until the characters' inner lives and private joys and problems are human and idiosyncratic, and as real to the director as his own. And it means reading the actors' impulses and feelings — including those that the actors themselves may not know they have.

A filmmaker's most precious assets — not just for directing actors, but for all the storytelling decisions — are his instincts, imagination, and intuition. Judith Weston gives away the secrets that can keep an imagination alive and free a director's intuition, so everyone on the set can function at full creativity.

Includes chapters on:
- Sources of Imagination.
- Goals of Script Analysis.
- Tools of the Storyteller.
- The Lost Art of Rehearsal.
- Director's Authority.
- Sample script analysis of scenes from *sex, lies, and videotape*; *Clerks*; and *Tender Mercies*.

"Judith's method is wonderful because it is practical. She has given me numerous tools to solve problems on the set and to earn the trust of actors. Her classes and her book are invaluable resources to any director."
> — *Lawrence Trilling, Director*
> *Nip/Tuck, Monk, Alias, Ed*

"Five stars! 10/10! A MUST SEE!!!"
> — *Nigel Dick, Director of Music Videos for*
> *Matchbox 20, Paul McCartney, R.E.M.,*
> *Guns N' Roses, Britney Spears, Ozzy Osbourne*

JUDITH WESTON is also the author of the best-selling book, *Directing Actors*.

$26.95 | 250 PAGES | ORDER # 111RLS | ISBN: 0-941188-78-7

THE WRITER'S JOURNEY
2ND EDITION
MYTHIC STRUCTURE FOR WRITERS

CHRISTOPHER VOGLER

BEST SELLER
OVER 116,500 UNITS SOLD!

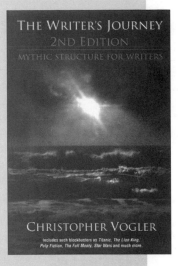

See why this book has become an international bestseller and a true classic. *The Writer's Journey* explores the powerful relationship between mythology and storytelling in a clear, concise style that's made it required reading for movie executives, screenwriters, playwrights, scholars, and fans of pop culture all over the world.

Both fiction and nonfiction writers will discover a set of useful myth-inspired storytelling paradigms (i.e., "The Hero's Journey") and step-by-step guidelines to plot and character development. Based on the work of Joseph Campbell, *The Writer's Journey* is a must for all writers interested in further developing their craft.

The updated and revised second edition provides new insights and observations from Vogler's ongoing work on mythology's influence on stories, movies, and man himself.

"This book is like having the smartest person in the story meeting come home with you and whisper what to do in your ear as you write a screenplay. Insight for insight, step for step, Chris Vogler takes us through the process of connecting theme to story and making a script come alive."

> — Lynda Obst, Producer
> Sleepless in Seattle, How to Lose a Guy in 10 Days
> *Author*, Hello, He Lied

"This is a book about the stories we write, and perhaps more importantly, the stories we live. It is the most influential work I have yet encountered on the art, nature, and the very purpose of storytelling."

> — Bruce Joel Rubin, Screenwriter
> Stuart Little 2, Deep Impact, Ghost, Jacob's Ladder

CHRISTOPHER VOGLER, a top Hollywood story consultant and development executive, has worked on such high-grossing feature films as *The Lion King*, *The Thin Red Line*, *Fight Club*, and *Beauty and the Beast*. He conducts writing workshops around the globe.

$24.95 | 325 PAGES | ORDER # 98RLS | ISBN: 0-941188-70-1

SETTING UP YOUR SHOTS
GREAT CAMERA MOVES EVERY FILMMAKER SHOULD KNOW

JEREMY VINEYARD

BEST SELLER
OVER 27,300 UNITS SOLD!

Written in straightforward, non-technical language and laid out in a nonlinear format with self-contained chapters for quick, on-the-set reference, *Setting Up Your Shots* is like a Swiss army knife for filmmakers! Using examples from over 140 popular films, this book provides detailed descriptions of more than 100 camera setups, angles, and techniques — in an easy-to-use horizontal "wide-screen" format.

Setting Up Your Shots is an excellent primer for beginning filmmakers and students of film theory, as well as a handy guide for working filmmakers. If you are a director, a storyboard artist, or an animator, use this book. It is the culmination of hundreds of hours of research.

Contains 150 references to the great shots from your favorite films, including *2001: A Space Odyssey*, *Blue Velvet*, *The Matrix*, *The Usual Suspects*, and *Vertigo*.

"Perfect for any film enthusiast looking for the secrets behind creating film. Because of its simplicity of design and straightforward storyboards, Setting Up Your Shots *is destined to be mandatory reading at film schools throughout the world."*
— *Ross Otterman*, Directed By Magazine

*"*Setting Up Your Shots *is a great book for defining the shots of today. The storyboard examples on every page make it a valuable reference book for directors and DPs alike! This great learning tool should be a boon for writers who want to choose the most effective shot and clearly show it in their boards for the maximum impact."*
— *Paul Clatworthy, Creator, StoryBoard Artist and StoryBoard Quick Software*

"This book is for both beginning and experienced filmmakers. It's a great reference tool, a quick reminder of the most commonly used shots by the greatest filmmakers of all time."
— *Cory Williams, President, Alternative Productions*

JEREMY VINEYARD is a filmmaker, internationally published author, and screenwriter. He is currently assembling a cast and crew for a crime feature to be shot in 2005.

$19.95 | 132 PAGES | ORDER # 8RLS | ISBN: 0-941188-73-6

24 HOURS | 1.800.833.5738 | WWW.MWP.COM

ORDER FORM

MICHAEL WIESE PRODUCTIONS
11288 VENTURA BLVD., # 621
STUDIO CITY, CA 91604
E-MAIL: MWPSALES@MWP.COM
WEB SITE: WWW.MWP.COM

WRITE OR FAX FOR A FREE CATALOG

PLEASE SEND ME THE FOLLOWING BOOKS:

TITLE	ORDER NUMBER (#RLS _____)	AMOUNT
_____	_____	_____
_____	_____	_____
_____	_____	_____
_____	_____	_____
_____	_____	_____

SHIPPING _____

CALIFORNIA TAX **(8.00%)** _____

TOTAL ENCLOSED _____

PLEASE MAKE CHECK OR MONEY ORDER PAYABLE TO:

MICHAEL WIESE PRODUCTIONS

(CHECK ONE) _____ MASTERCARD _____ VISA _____ AMEX

CREDIT CARD NUMBER _____

EXPIRATION DATE _____

CARDHOLDER'S NAME _____

CARDHOLDER'S SIGNATURE _____

SHIP TO:

NAME _____

ADDRESS _____

CITY _____ STATE _____ ZIP _____

COUNTRY _____ TELEPHONE _____